DI051985

To Penelope
My partner in life and travel.

THE GRA

2 Gizeh, Pyramids of Cheops, 2250 BC
builder: Cheops

The very icons of ancient Egypt, these giant minimal sculptures stand in a sandy desert area near Cairo. The largest is 146,6 m high on a square base of 230 m, built of solid limestone blocks weighing some 2 tons each. The pyramid contains the King's, and below it, the Queen's burial chambers near its centre, reached by an internal sloping grand gallery, made of granite. Originally, the pyramids were covered in finely finished limestone with the peak reputed to have been covered in gold. All of this, however, was pillaged over the centuries.

3 Philae, Temple of Isis, 330 BC
Rebuilt on high ground to avoid dam inundation.

4 Edfu, Temple of Horus, 237-57 BC
The great Pylon-Portico has the characteristically tapered profile of a number of temples, which gives lateral stability to the 30 m high structure. A beautifully proportioned entrance is topped by a stone tieing element and opens onto an internal colonnaded court leading to the inner sanctum of the temple.

5 Sakkara, 3000 BC
Entrance into a palace court with beautifully proportioned opening and recesses in the masonry surface.

6 Karnak, Temple of Amun
Incised figures and hieroglyphics on a limestone wall.

7 Karnak, Temple of Amun
Entry into the Hypostyle Hall flanked by huge granite figures.

8 Karnak, Temple of Amun, 1550 BC
Hypostyle Hall with closely spaced huge columns, incised with figures and hieroglyphics.

5

6

16

9

10

11

12

9 Temple at Edfu, 237-57 BC

10 Luxor Temple
Head of Ramesses II.

11 Edfu, 237-57 BC
Granite figure of Horus at the entry to the Temple at Edfu.

12 Luxor Temple
Entry of Temple with seated figures and obelisk. The missing right side obelisk was taken to France in the 19th Century and erected on the Place de la Concorde (see France photo 47).

13 Philae, Temple of Isis, 330 BC
The Temple was raised and rebuilt faithfully on a high ground island prior to the flooding of the Aswan Dam. The symmetrical portico structure is reminiscent of other Temples, but visual enticement is created in the opposing irregular spatial disposition of the arcaded forecourt wings. Beautiful, ever-changing spaces result as one walks through the complex.

14, 17 Nubia, Abu Simbel
The raised and rebuilt giant rock hewn sculptures of Ramses II.

15 Nubia, Kalabsha Temple
The rebuilt Temple on high ground is only reachable by water.

16 Esna, Chnum-Temple
The Temple stands in a town and is surrounded by buildings. It is smaller than others with a colonnade enclosed by screen walls.

18 Gizeh, The Sphinx, 2500 BC
Damaged over centuries, it still represents an unforgettable image of a human head with an animal's body.

19 Thebes, Temple of Queen Hatshepsut, 1550 BC
Architect: Senenmut
The setting of this terraced mortuary temple is spectacular. Rising from the Nile Valley it is approached by ramps to 3 levels toward the base of dramatic high rock cliffs. Double colonnades surround walled courts with fine incised relief sculptures.

14

15

16

17

18

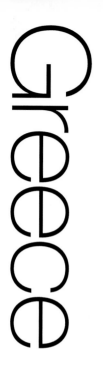

Greece

The rich legacy of ancient Greece between 500-300 BC, formed the fountainhead of western civilisation; in the arts, in literature, skills of government, but especially in the influence of its refined architecture. The design of temple buildings contained such subtle depth of aesthetic sensibility as to become the prototypes of important buildings and monuments for the next 2,500 years. This heritage can rightfully be called "International Style" as against that term often used erroneously to describe 20th Century architecture, which changes constantly and is not a style.

Greek Architecture has been recorded and studied, particularly the optical refinements of temple facades, which were repeated for centuries on important buildings throughout most of the civilised world. The finest celebrated ancient examples are the sanctuary buildings on the Acropolis in Athens. They contain the visual adjustments devised to combat optical illusions and achieve a "corrected" view of reality for the onlooker. Marble column shafts were tapered toward the top to appear straighter and more graceful to the eye. Building bases were convex in the centre to look more horizontal and the spacing of portico end columns was made closer so as to appear more equal with the adjoining group, etc. Column designs followed one of three main "Orders", the simplest being Doric, with fluted sharp arrised grooves, Ionic having voluted scroll capitals and Corinthian sculptured in the form of Acanthus leaves. Our eyes are fully attuned to seeing these ubiquitous Greek forms on buildings, which have been a prescribed style in certain periods of history. Construction of such buildings is highly labour intensive and virtually impossible to replicate today, and yet many people still feel comfortable and relate to them in preference to much of the architecture of our own time.

In more recent centuries, the architecture and urban fabric on the multitude of Greek Islands developed from the use of arches and domes especially in the celebrated steep hillside towns of Mykonos and Santorini.

1

1 Erectheion, 421-406 BC
Supporting Caryatid statue of a young
maiden, Erectheum, Athens.

2

3

2 Athens, Parthenon, 440 BC
Architects: Ictinus and Callicrates
The Parthenon temple of Athena,
considered the most perfect of classic
buildings in antiquity.

3 Athens, Erectheion, 421-406 BC
Architect: Mnesicles
An irregular building on the Acropolis with
an attached porch supported by Caryatids,
sculpted figures of young maidens instead
of columns.

4 Athens, Propylaea, 437-432 BC
The entrance portico to the Acropolis.

5 Athens, Acropolis
Built on a platformed mountain.

6

7

6 Athens, Temple of Athena, Nike Apteros, 427-424 BC
Architect: Callicrates
The small structure defies regularity by being placed at an angle, resulting in a dynamic spatial relationship with the adjacent Propylaea..

7 Sounion, Temple of Poseidon, 440 BC
Built on a dramatic promontory east of Athens overlooking the Aegean Sea.

8 Delphi, Amphitheatre
As many other Greek theatres, the semi-circular seating is built into the natural slope of the land and overlooks the splendid mountain setting.

9 Delphi
The circular temple structure at the bottom of a sloping site.

9

10,13,14 Santorini
The steep hillside overlooks the Aegean Sea.

11 Mikonos
Narrow streets with white painted walls and paving.

12 Mikonos
The ancient wind driven flour mill is still in use after centuries.

15 Oia
A Church high up above the sea.

16 Athens
Son et luminaire performance at the Acropolis.

10

11

12

13

14

15

Italy

If there is one country and its people that
have contributed most to western civilisation's man-made world continuously for
the last 2000 years, it must surely be Italy.
Starting with the vast Roman Empire, its
colonising tentacles reaching most of
Europe, there are the daring engineering
structures: the architectural form language
was inherited from the ancient Greeks, but
the application into huge structures that
bear testimony to their intuitive engineering,
are handed down to us, mostly intact to
this day. The Romans were not inventors
of the supporting arch, but its extended
use in vaults and intersecting barrel shapes
and domes is theirs. Structures such as the
Pantheon in Rome or the impressive aqueducts they built, the Pont du Gard in France
and at Segovia in Spain, the huge public
baths, stadia and theatres, boggles the
mind today, just to think that they were
based on experimental, empirical knowl-
edge without the mathematical systems
of analysis that we know today.
In the Middle Ages, Italian towns grew not
with a clear devised plan, but an organic
assembly of tightly packed environments
with narrow streets that burst open into
most delightful public plazas that are the
joy of inhabitants as much as to the envying
hoards of tourists that frequent and travel
through Italy, it seems continuously. After
about the first Millennium, Italy was the
cradle of Romanesque architecture, which
spread throughout Europe, much of it
extending the structural daring with minimal visual elaboration.
Borne out of this, starting around the 17th
Century was the Baroque era. It is my
view that it is one of the architectural peak
periods in western civilisation. The structural
scheme of domed support was refined into
spatially complex and daring backgrounds
for the visual exuberance of painting and
sculpture that adorn the period's celebrated
works. My favourite is Borromini and his
masterful Quattro Fontane and St. Ivo
church interiors that combined a structural
virtuosity achieved with geometrically minimal means in contrast to his exuberant rival
Bernini, best known for his brilliant sculp-

tures and elaborate fountains which are dotted throughout Rome – or Guarini's buildings in Turin. It is still Borromini's structural inventions that have most to say to us to this day in that they show arched interiors whose ribs elements narrow and deepen toward the top of domes, recognising intuitively that greater stiffness is needed there. This is confirmed by today's method of structural analysis. However, the mode of the Baroque era, aside from structural innovation, were the decorative embellishments which endear that time and have never ceased to fascinate and delight the visitor, such as Pozzo's magnificent frescos in St Ignacio. He remained in demand beyond Italy, as was the muralist Tiepolo. The period's structural inventiveness bore fruit, was repeated and extended by the great engineer-architect Balthazar Neumann in 18th Century Germany (see Germany photos 13-15). The late Pier Luigi Nervi, in our time, is Borromini's structural descendent. He represents the highpoint of 20th Century expressive engineering. His structures are not only mathematically and constructionally logical, but deeply satisfying aesthetically in that the static laws of nature are made evident and are given form without any painterly or sculptural embellishments – such as in his Olympic Stadia structures of the 1960s.

1

1 Rome, Circular Temple of Portunus 1st Century AD, by the Tiber.

3

4

2-4 Paestum, Temple of Neptune, 500 BC
The early best preserved Greek Temples.
The Doric columns in the centre are heavier
than later ones and are in superimposed
two tiers.

**5 Pompeii, Patrician's House,
2nd Century AD**
Interior courtyard.

6 Rome, Colosseum, 70-82 AD
The most magnificent of many Roman amphitheatres, accommodated 60,000 spectators in an amazing engineering feat for its time.

7 Taormina Theatre
The originally Greek and later Roman Theatre overlooks the beautiful coast of Sicily.

8-10 Rome, The Pantheon, 118-126 AD
The circular building has the same diameter and height of about 50 m – an engineering triumph built in successively diminishing rings of stone with an open oculus in the centre.

11 Rome, The Pantheon, 118-126 AD
Exterior of the portico.

7

8

9

10

12

13

14

15

16

17

12 Pisa, Dom St. Maria Assunta and The Leaning Tower, 12th Century

13 Venice, St Mark's, 13th Century
Campanili rebuilt after collapse in 1902.

14 Siena, Palazzo Publico Tower, 1300
Overlooking the public plaza. Famous for its yearly horse race, the Palio.

15 Bologna, Brick Towers, 1100
Torre Asinelli and Garisenda.

16, 17 San Gimignano
The Tuscan hill town has high brick towers built by ruling families in the 10th and 11th Century. Their purpose is unclear and may have been for protection, storage, or simply rivalry between families to build high.

18 Apulia, Castel del Monte, 1240-50
Built by Fredrick II as a hunting castle, the building has a crystal clear octagonal symmetrical form with identical trapezoidal rooms on two floors. At its centre is an open courtyard.

19-21 Mondavio
In the Marche area of eastern Italy are 15th
Century fortified hill towns surrounded by
high walls of brick. The "Rocca" defence
towers are of extraordinary geometric
shapes corbelling outward at the top.

22 Senegalia
The fortifications on the Adriatic Coast.

19

20

21

22

52

23 Orvieto, Cathedral, 1290-1500
Architect: Arnolfo di Cambio.
Has a quasi-Gothic façade decorated with colourful mosaics.

24 Rome, Tempietto, 1502
Architect: Donato Bramante
A High Renaissance small circular domed temple is built in the cloister of S. Pietro in Montorio.

25 Florence, S. Maria Novella, 1300
Architect: Leon Battista Alberti
The Renaissance façade of 1460.

26 Mantua, S. Andrea, 1470-76
Architect Leon Battista Alberti
The deeply recessed arched entry is one of the earliest Renaissance structures.

27 Venice, S. Zaccaria, 1450
Has a deeply moulded façade with beautiful arched roof forms.

28 Venice, Scuola di San Marco, 1490
Highlights of the arched elements of the façade are on either side of the entrance portals. Pictorial compositions in coloured marbles create perspective scenes, which appear to have a third dimension in depth.

23

24

25

26

27

28

29 Rome, Piazza del Popolo, 1670
Architect: C. Rainaldi
The central obelisk marks the converging point of three streets, flanked by two domed churches.

30 Rome, Piazza Navona, 1600's
Francesco Borromini's concave façade of the Sant' Agnese Church.

31 Florence, Ponte Veccio, 1345

37

32 Florence, Pitti Palace, 1460

33 Siena, 12th Century
Medieval tight network of narrow streets.

34 Siena Piazza del Campo, 14th Cent.
The open Campo, focus of the city.

35 Stra, Palace Pisani, 18th Century
The theatrical façade is merely a stable.

36 Venice, St Marks Square
The grandest urban space in Europe.

38

37 Rome, Piazza del Campidoglio, 1538
Architect: Michelangelo
The three buildings defining the trapezoidal plaza are placed apart to defy perspective and appear parallel.

38 Florence, Pazzi Chapel, 1429-61
Architect: Filippo Brunelleschi

39 Lucca
The oval-shaped central space follows the form of an ancient Roman amphitheatre.

39

40 Vigevano, 1492
Attributed to Donato Bramante. The painted facades reputed to be by Leonardo da Vinci.

42

41 Caserta, Royal Palace 1752
Architect: Luigi Vanvitelli
The grand staircase in the octagonal
vestibule creates multiple vistas in several
directions.

42 Turin, San Lorenzo, 1668-87
Architect: Guarino Guarini
Based on octagonal geometrics the plan
ends in a top-lit dome supported by eight
interlocking ribs.

44

43 Venice, Santa Maria della Salute, 1630
Architect: Baldassare Longhena

44 Venice, Ca' d'Oro, 1430
Architects: Giovanni & Bartolommeo Buon

45 Venice, San Giorgio Maggiore, 1560-80
Architect: Andrea Palladio

46

47

48

46 Maser, Villa Barbaro, 1550
Architect: Andrea Palladio
A combined country house with farm buildings.

47 Maser, Villa Barbaro, 1550
Architect: Andrea Palladio
Interior. The central wing has life-size wall frescos by Paolo Veronese.

48 Vicenza, Basilica, 1549
Architect: Andrea Palladio
The façade with the typical "Palladian" motive of Serliana openings of arches and columns.

49 Fanzolo, Villa Emo, 1565
Architect: Andrea Palladio
As with Villa Barbaro, a combined residence with arcaded access wings.

50 Urbino, 1450
The fortress-like palace of the Duke Federico da Montefeltro dominates the dramatic walled hill town.

51

51 Rome, St Peter's Piazza, 1656-1667
Architect: Gian Lorenzo Bernini
An appropriate setting for large crowds of
pilgrims enclosed by huge semi-circular
colonnades scaled to relate to the façade
of St Peters.

52 Gian Lorenzo Bernini, 1598-1680

53 Rome, St. Peters
Detail of the encircling colonnade's columns.

**54 Rome, St. Peters Basilica, 16th and
17th Century**
Designed successively by a number of
Architects, Donato Bramante, Michelangelo
and Carlo Maderno. The focus of the
enormous interior is Bernini's Baldachino
supported by twisted bronze columns
(looted from the Pantheon) under the great
dome.

55 Rome, St. Peters Basilica Plan

53

54

Harry Seidler   Travelling the World with an Architect's Eye

ND TOUR

TASCHEN

KÖLN LONDON LOS ANGELES MADRID PARIS TOKYO

Front cover, top:
Braga (Portugal), Bom Jesus do Monte,
18th Century
Front cover, bottom:
Barcelona (Spain), German Pavilion, 1929
Back cover, top:
Niterói (Brazil), Contemporary Art Museum,
1996
Back cover, bottom:
Córdoba (Spain), Great Mosque, 9–10th
Century

© 2003 TASCHEN GmbH
Hohenzollernring 53, D–50672 Köln
www.taschen.com

All rights reserved. No part of this
publication may be reproduced, stored
in a retrieval system, or transmitted in
any form or by any means, electronic,
mechanical, photocopying, recording,
or otherwise, without prior consent of
the publishers.

© 2003 VG Bild-Kunst, Bonn, for the
works of Luis Barragan, Peter Behrens,
Victor Horta, Le Corbusier, Adolf Loos,
Gerrit Rietveld, Ludwig Mies van der Rohe
and Frank Lloyd Wright.

Designed by Massimo Vignelli
Translation by Latido, Bremen

Printed in Italy
ISBN 3–8228–2555–7

Contents

Introduction

This book aims to portray the peak achievements in architecture and the built environment that I have seen, all around the globe. The photos were taken by me over a period in excess of 50 years and show in juxtaposition the work of 3000 BC, up to the latest buildings of our own time. My predisposition to travel started involuntarily at the age of 15 in my native Vienna, which I left following the Anschluss in 1938. After a 10 year circuitous Odyssey from internment in England and Canada to studies there and the USA, to work in Brazil, I finally settled in Australia and commenced practice of architecture in 1948.

After some years, circumnavigation of the globe started with ever increasing frequency - to experience the most celebrated ancient and current architecture in Europe, Asia and America.

With frequent stops in Rome to consult with the engineer Pier Luigi Nervi on my concrete structures, I first experienced the impact of historic architecture in any depth. Developing what I call a passive appreciation and respect for the great building achievements of the past - I saw this as a simultaneous active love and dedication to developing an appropriate architecture, expressive of the artistic and technological impacts in building today. One can appreciate traditional architecture in relation to its period, the given circumstances of man's artistic aspirations, technical means and the social-political conditions of the time, as against the involved, active enthusiasm evoked by the masterpieces of the time in which one builds.

The ease and speed of jet travel opened up the world in the 1960's. The frequent visits to Rome were extended later involving trips to my buildings during construction in Paris, Mexico, Hong Kong and recently in my hometown of Vienna. In addition, teaching and lecturing in many countries amplified this routine to long distance flying 3 and 4 times a year, always with time for photography, recording the delight I felt seeing township environments and the icon buildings of all eras.

© Photo: Penelope Seidler

The extensive assembly of images aims to be of international interest equally to the lay public, architects, students of architecture and historians, in the hope that they will be encouraged to travel and seek out what I feel to be much of the finest man has built in our time and throughout recorded history.

My photographer brother, Marcell (1919-1977) gave me simple advice when I started to record architectural sites "Only use Leica cameras and Kodachrome film, which is archival". I have adhered to this in taking all images in this book, some over 50 years ago.

Egypt

Egypt's antiquity has always stood out as unique in comparison to other cultures anywhere on the globe. What makes it so special are the works handed down to us, their gargantuan size, built millennia ago of solid stone; the pyramids, obelisks, temples, sculptures and artworks. It seems inconceivable to visualise how these enormous works, such as 250 ton stone obelisks, were physically brought into existence, extracted and erected, with the minimal technical means available, 5,000 years ago.

Spread along the fertile Nile River Valley, these great structures are spaced on both sides of the river. It was all developed by people with the longest lasting stable civilisation in antiquity.

Ruled over by autocratic kings who were worshipped as divine royalty, they had huge works built as visible memorials, such as burial chambers contained in the great pyramids, colossal statues of their images and left evidence of the enrichment in their lives through luxury articles and solid gold masks found in their tombs.

As an outstanding example, the God-King, Pharaoh Ramses II, built the Temple to the God Amun at Karnak, with closely spaced sandstone columns some 25 m high and 3 m in diameter. The capitals are of Lotus form, covered with incised figures and hieroglyphics in the Hypostyle Hall, which is lit from above through clerestory openings. The surfaces of depository limestone or sandstone walls and columns have inevitably deteriorated and fretted away with time. The ancient Egyptians must have been well aware of this because when it came to sculpturing the images of their Gods, such as the Falcon Bird Horus, or the heads of Pharaohs, they used igneous stone such as solid granite.

Horus made of Aswan black granite has been standing exposed to the elements flanking the entrance of the Temple at Edfu for the last 3,500 years. It is in perfect condition, with edges sharp and features undisturbed. Whenever today's salesmen of new technology materials claim that their products will stand the test of time, I prefer to believe in the irrevocable evidence offered by Horus in choosing exterior materials for my buildings.

The form language used by the ancient Egyptians in their structures is minimal. The silhouettes read distinctively and powerfully even from a distance. It is only when approaching that one becomes aware of the human figures and hiero-glyphics incised in them, which gives richness to the geometric forms. The characteristic outwardly tapered Temple walls shows evidence of an intuitive re-sponse to the need for lateral structural stability and resistance to earthquakes. The benign frost-free climate of Egypt contributes to the remarkable condition in which these structures have survived for millennia.

With the construction of the Aswan high dam in the 1960's, numerous ancient monuments and temples were threatened with inundation. Under the initiative of UNESCO, some of them were saved by being moved and reconstructed on higher ground. The most dramatic of these raisings were the Abu Simbel Colossal sculptures of Ramses II, which were rebuilt against an artificially constructed mountain with a final appearance identical to the original.

1

1 Karnak, temple of Amun, 1550 BC

57

56 Rome, Piazza Navona "Four Rivers" Fountain, 1648-51
Architect: Gian Lorenzo Bernini
The fountain is fed by water from restored ancient aqueducts. It is placed in front of St Agnese, the concave fronted Church built by his architectural rival, Borromini.

57 Rome, The Chapel in the Collegio di Propaganda Fide, 1660
Architect: F. Borromini
The interlocking ceiling ribs emanating from the four corners of the hall indicate an early awareness of structural forces (see page 84).

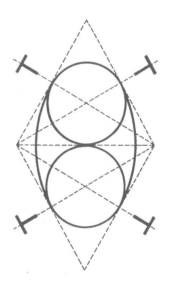

60 Francesco Borromini, 1599-1667

58, 59, 61 Rome, S. Carlo alle Quattro Fontane, 1638-41

Architect: Francesco Borromini

Even though small in scale, this Church is a most celebrated masterpiece of early Baroque architecture. Its pulsating, undulating façade is unique for its period. Based on clear geometric themes of related circles and ellipses, which are carried to the interior, they display an intuitive response to structural forces.

The interior of the dome is composed of three geometric coffer forms, said to be symbolic of the Trinity. They diminish in size toward the top, thereby increasing the apparent height of the dome in perspective. What is more is the increased stiffness, resulting from closer spaced ribs at the top, to resist the bending forces where they are greatest.

This building represents a rare simultaneous architectural solution to symbolic requirements, geometric-structural needs and aesthetic fulfilment of the totality.

63

62-64 Rome, S. Ivo alla Sapienza, 1642-50
Architect: Francesco Borromini
The plan forms a six pointed star with ends alternately convex and concave curves. These are carried up to the base of the dome. The geometry changes and transforms toward the top into a circular oculus, which supports the lantern.

64

65, 66 Rome, S. Maria Della Pace, 1656-57
Architect: Pietro da Cortona
The projecting form of the Church increases the apparent size of the small surrounding urban square. Opposing convex and concave quadrant shaped curves give both horizontally and vertically give the Church and Square a dynamic image.

67 Rome, Collegio di Propaganda Fide, 1660
Architect: Francesco Borromini
The concave-convex entrance façade.

68 Rome, S. Ignacio Church, 1691
Fresco by Fra Andrea Pozzo
The huge illusionary painting creates the perspective impression of great height.

69 Rome, Piazza S. Ignacio, 1727
Architect: Filippo Raguzzini
The oval shape of the stage like setting plaza is created by the concave facades of surrounding buildings.

71

70 Rome, The Spanish Steps, 1723-26
Architect: Francesco de Sanctis
Leading up to the Trinita dei Monti Church, the steps are usually full of sitting people overlooking the popular square with its marble barge shaped fountain by Bernini.

71 Tivoli Fountains of Villa D'este, 1570
The spectacular water display is character-istic of the period's aim for dramatic effects.

72 Alberobello, Trulli Stone Houses
Due to the lack of available timber, these houses have conical roofs constructed with circular layers of stone slabs reducing in size toward to apex.

73

75

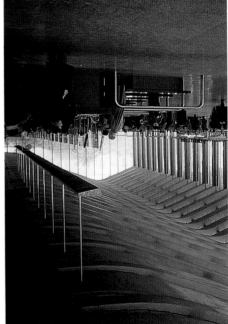

73 Como, Casa del Fascio, 1936
Architect: Giuseppe Terragni
A pure and minimalistic example of Italian modern architecture, with a beautifully proportioned façade and spatial interiors.

74, 76 Bologna, L'Esprit Nouveau Pavilion
Architect: Le Corbusier
Reconstructed by the City of Bologna in a park, the exhibition building was first built for the 1925 Paris display. It contains a furnished maisonette apartment, the prototype for the 1947 Unité d'Habitation in Marseille. In an attached wing are top lit dioramas of Le Corbusier's concept drawings for his ideal city "Ville Radiense".

75 Rome, Railway Station, 1950
The entrance hall is given great height by upwardly shaped concrete roof beams, which form a projecting portico on the exterior.

79

77, 78 Turin, Palace of Labour, 1960
Architect: Pier Luigi Nervi
The cantilevered steel roof beams are
supported by expressively tapered concrete
columns.

79 Mantua, Burgo Paper Mill, 1961
Architect: Pier Luigi Nervi
The 165 m span suspension structure is
carried by concrete trestles.

80 Pier Luigi Nervi, 1891-1979

80

81 Rome, Palazzetto dello Sport, 1957
Architect: Pier Luigi Nervi
This smaller of the two Olympic Stadia built
for the 1960 Games was constructed of
precast "ferro cement" pans, a system
invented by Nervi, to form interlocking
concrete ribs poured between them to
span large distances.
The building represents a rare fusion of
rational structure with a sculpturally
satisfying aesthetic result.

Germany lost many of its architectural treasures during World War II (such as through the senseless bombing of Dresden). However, great buildings and environments in country areas and small towns remain and have mostly been painstakingly restored. The highlights are medieval towns with half timber buildings and charming squares, but particularly the palaces and churches of the Baroque era. Many of these are centred in the south east of the country, which came to be called "Pfaffenwinkel" (Parsons' corner), such as the churches Wies, Ettal, Ottobeuren, etc.

The work of the 18th Century architect Balthasar Neumann (originally a military engineer), is especially known for his pilgrimage church of Vierzehnheiligen (Fourteen Saints). It is a splendid Rococo building with interlocking twisted profile ribs supporting the wide masonry roof vaults. After a mid-19th Century fire in the timber roof, the structure was found to contain embedded iron bars in the stone and concrete vaults and ribs. I believe this to be the earliest and intuitive use of the principle of "reinforced concrete". The white ceiling and its exuberantly colourful frescoes remained intact after the fire.

Germany's unique contribution to architecture dates from the pioneering developments of the 1920's and 30's. Centred in the establishment by Walter Gropius of the "Bauhaus" in Weimar 1919 and later in Dessau 1925, that teaching and experimental institution has had a continuing influence in architecture, industrial design and art throughout most of the world to this day.

The principles developed at the Bauhaus were aimed to bring into unison, consideration of practical need, advanced technology and the art of the time, into a Total Work of Art (Gesamtkunstwerk). Its far reaching influence is to be seen throughout the civilised world. The resulting forms of design remain in perpetual flux. They will change with time, responding to altered needs, advances in technology and developments in art. The many celebrated 20th Century buildings in different countries give

Germany

evidence of the fact that Modern archi-tecture cannot be called a "style" of fixed design characteristics.
The methodology developed at the German Bauhaus remains valid with the passage of time.

1

1 Bamberg, Cathedral, 1215-37
The Gothic ribbed vaulted nave.

2 Rothenburg ob der Tauber
The pedestrian area in the medieval town centre.

4

5

3 Rothenburg ob der Tauber
The arch and tower over the original town gate.

4 Bamberg, Town Hall, 1461-67
The Town Hall built on an island in the River Regnitz.

5 Bamberg, Town Hall, 1750
The Baroque balcony on the transformed central wing of the Town Hall.

6 Munich, Nymphenburg Palace, 1730
Architect: Joseph Effner
The summer palace in its park setting.

9

7

8

7-9 Munich, The Amalienburg, 1735
Architect: François de Cuvilliés
Built in the park surrounding the Nymphen-
burg as a hunting lodge. Mozart is reputed
to have performed in the Rococo white
and elaborately silver and blue decorated
Spiegel Saal (Mirror Hall).

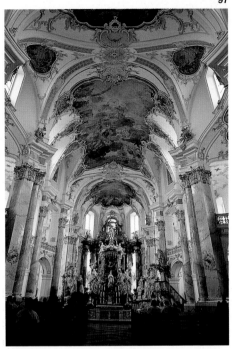

11

10-12 Vierzehnheiligen (Fourteen Saints), 1750

Architect: Balthasar Neumann
with the Monastery of Banz in the distance
(by Johann L. Dienztenhofer). The pilgrimage
church is a supreme example of Rococo
architecture in Germany. The comparatively
quiet exterior bursts forth on the interior
into a brilliant assembly of frescoed oval
and elliptical vaults.

12

14

13-15 Vierzehnheiligen, 1750

Architect: Balthasar Neumann

The luminous quality of the interior results from the light admitted from large windows, reflected from a white structure in contrast to the colourful fresco paintings. The structural ingenuity of the building is evident at the "Vierung", the interaction of four vaults at their merging. The twisted surfaces of the supporting ribs are reminiscent of Pier Luigi Nervi's structures of 200 years later.

6

17

16 Neresheim, Monastery, 1745-64
Architect: Balthasar Neumann

17, 20 Munich, S. Johann Nepomuk, (Asamkirche), 1733-46
Architects: Asam Brothers
Built on a narrow city site, this Rococo Church is riotously decorated with undulating forms without any surface left plain.

18, 19, 22, 23 Würzburg, Residenz Palace, 1750
Architect: Balthasar Neumann (and others)
The Chapel and Emperor's halls with frescoes by the celebrated Venetian painter Giovanni Battista Tiepolo.
The grand staircase of 1735 with the ceiling fresco also by Tiepolo are the most satis-fying and grandiose works of German Baroque.

21 Weltenburg, 1716-39
Architects: Asam Brothers
This Benedictine abbey is distinguished by indirect natural light from above, with the effect of intense artificial spotlighting falling on the focal altar and central sculpture of St. George and the dragon. The impact is that of a dramatic stage setting.

24 Neresheim, Monastery, 1745
Architect: Balthasar Neumann

25

26

27

25 Dresden, Opera, 1878
Architect: Gottfried Semper
Badly damaged during World War II, but
reconstructed faithfully.

26, 27 Dresden, Zwinger, 1710-28
Architect: Matthäus Daniel Pöppelmann
The suspended gilded crown dome over
the entrance to the complex across a
bridge.

28

28-30 Potsdam, Sanssouci, 1745
Architect: Georg Wenzeslaus von Knobelsdorff
Built as a retreat for Fredrick the Great, the approach is through a semi-circular colonnade into a long, one-storey pavilion with a sumptuously furnished domed oval hall. On the view side, a grand stair leads down to a large fountain flanked by terraced orangeries and vineyards.

29

30

31

32

33

34

35

31, 32 Berlin, AEG Turbine Hall, 1908
Architect: Peter Behrens
A pioneering industrial steel structure with riveted exposed columns on pivoted supports.

33, 34 Alfeld, Faguswerke, 1911
Architect: Walter Gropius
A glass "curtain wall" building revolutionary for its time, covering the floors and structure, except for the expressed columns.

35 Walter Gropius 1883 -1969

36

36, 39 Dessau, Bauhaus, 1925
Architect: Walter Gropius
Not only did this building house an institute developing a new approach to architecture, industrial design and art, but it is a famous example of architecture expressive in its parts of diverse purposes.
The workshop wing is fully glazed for maximum daylight. Classroom wings have continuous horizontal ribbon windows; the "Prellerhaus" students' studio and living quarters have individual balconies, etc.

37, 38 Dessau, Bauhaus, 1925
Examples of innovative industrial design; exposed and connected fluorescent tubes on the ceiling in patterns recalling abstract paintings of the time.
The tubular steel folding theatre seating designed by Marcel Breuer.

37

38

40 Berlin, Gropiusstadt, 1963-73
Architect: Walter Gropius
A huge housing development in an open park setting with low, medium and high-rise structures.

41 Berlin, 1927
The residence of architect Erich Mendelsohn.

42 Berlin, Neue National Gallery, 1968
Architect: Mies van der Rohe.

43 Frankfurt, Modern Art Museum 1987-90
Architect: Hans Hollein
The building takes on the shape of its triangular site. On the interior new concepts of spatial interplay dominate.

44, 45 Munich, Olympic Site, 1972
Architect: Frei Otto
A covering structure of plastic panels is suspended from metal poles. The huge hanging roof seems to deny conventional concepts of gravity.

46 Weil-am-Rhein, Vitra Design Museum, 1989
Architect: Frank Gehry
The unconventional geometry defying regular repetitive structure evolved from computer equipment to generate and produce any shape of structural elements. The large entrance sculpture depicting carpentry tools is by Claes Oldenburg.

47 Stuttgart, Weissenhof Siedlung 1927
Architect: Le Corbusier
Duplex Housing in the influential Deutscher Werkbund Housing Display.

48-51 Bonn, Kunstmuseum, 1985-93
Architect: Axel Schultes
Its architecture maximises spatial effects by fusing areas horizontally and vertically.

52 Brühl, Augustusburg, 1740-61
Architect: Balthasar Neumann
designed the main staircase and Carlone painted most of the ceiling frescoes.

40

41

42

43

44

45

46

47

France

The development of architecture in France reached many high points throughout history. From the ancient Roman province of Gallia, some daring engineering structures remain, such as the Pont du Gard, a 50 m high aqueduct built 2,000 years ago of unadorned three tier supporting stone arches.

The Romanesque era in the 11th and 12th Centuries produced unique churches and fortified towns. A peak was reached in the Gothic period when dramatic cathedrals with majestic stained glass windows were built higher and wider than any others in Europe; such as at Beauvais. The structural ingenuity achieving such huge enclosed spaces by means of thin stone piers stabilised by double flying buttresses is truly admirable.

The 16th Century saw elaborate fortified palatial chateaus built by the aristocracy in beautiful natural settings, often surrounded by water. The 17th Century was the era of sumptuous chateaus extended into manmade monumental formal gardens with axial vistas as far as the eye can see. One of the most brilliant is Veaule-Viconte, which was built for a State Minister under Louis XIV, Nicolas Fouquet, who commissioned the architect Le Veau, the garden architect Le-Notre and interiors by Lebrun. The King, invited to the extravagant house's opening celebration became furious that one of his Ministers dared to outdo him with such a sumptuous establishment. He ordered the house closed, put Fouquet in prison and commandeered his team of designers to build him such a palace, only bigger and better. The result was Versailles. Bigger and sumptuous it is, but not as exquisite aesthetically.

In prison, Fouquet was often visited by his architects, but never recovered from his misfortunes. He died 19 years later.

With the advent of the industrial revolution, the great rebuilding of Paris took place in the middle of the 19th Century under Napoleon III and his town planner, Haussmann. The grandeur of the Boulevards and axes of Paris, admired to this day, was made possible by the vision of this powerful Emperor and his architect. Their plans cut through the congested medieval parts of the city to give it more light and air, but also serve a strategic purpose of allowing unhindered military movement to quell citizen revolts. Following the technological and industrial advances made in England, the combination of iron structures, machines and the ambition to display the new means in the Paris world exhibition of 1889, produced some remarkable buildings. The icons of the time at the end of the 19th Century were huge assemblies of cast iron elements, such as the Eiffel Tower. It took a long time to give true visual expression to the potential of the new materials. Initially, the vaulted forms of traditional masonry architecture and even plant decorations were imitated, made out of iron. In the early years of the 20th Century the transient fashion of Art Nouveau used decorative curvilinear forms made of cast iron in stair railings and for entries to new underground stations of the Paris Metro.

The most significant new development for our own time took place about the end of World War I. Stimulated by the new art of the time such as the work of Cubist painters, architecture employed not only innovative technology and materials, but responded to the emerging new demands on buildings expected to be satisfied in a rational way.

Leading in this, from the 1920's onward, was the great architect, Le Corbusier. He devoted his time to painting in the morning and architecture in the afternoon. His prolific output in all related spheres, in paintings, building, visionary town planning schemes, and furniture, are without equal. It is impossible for an architect working in the 20th Century and today to claim that he is not influenced in some way, by Le Corbusier's visions and executed work. Together with Gropius, Mies van der Rohe and Frank Lloyd Wright, France's Le Corbusier is the greatest of these recognised "form givers" in architecture, whose work is beyond fashion and remains valid practically and visually, to this day.

1

1 Paris, Trocadero
View from the Eiffel Tower

118

2

2 Nimes, Pont du Gard, 19 BC
A spectacular Roman aqueduct engineering
feat 50 m high. The supporting arch
structure remains unadorned to serve
purely its utilitarian purpose.

3 Poitiers, Notre-Dame-la-Grande, 1140
A Romanesque masterpiece with a
sculptured entrance façade, conical turrets
and dome.

4 Paris, Notre-Dame Cathedral, started
1163
The high nave is braced by double span
flying buttresses. Large circular transept
stained glass windows are held by thin
stone tracery.

5 Beauvais Cathedral 1220 started, completed in the 16th Century

At 50 m it is the highest and widest of Gothic Cathedrals, plagued by structural failures and rebuilding during the long construction period. Only the apse end remains, which is awe inspiring with high clerestory windows.

6 Vézelay, S. Madeleine, 1089-1206

Romanesque Church with a high unadorned two-tone semi-circular stone arched nave.

7, 8 Chartres Cathedral, 1220

The building with two unequal height towers is made famous by the magnificent predominantly blue stained glass windows.

9, 10 Paris, Sainte-Chapelle, 1240

Architect: Pierre de Montrevil

A small court chapel, but very high for its width, almost entirely of 15 m high stained glass. The vaulted ceiling is decorated bright blue.

11 Carcassonne

A fortified medieval town containing a castle, churches and a theatre. Fallen into disrepair it was restored in the 19th Century by Architect Viollet-le-Duc.

5

6

7
8
9
10

126

12, 14 Carcassonne
A fortified medieval town containing a castle, churches and a theatre. Fallen into disrepair it was restored in the 19th Century by Architect Viollet-le-Duc.

13, 15 Albi Cathedral, 1280-1390
A fortress-like brick structure with projecting round piers. Attached to its side entrance, a finely ribbed Gothic portico was added which creates a fascinating contrast to the ponderous main building.

12

13

14

15

128

16

17

16, 17 Toulouse, Les Jacobins, 1260
The early Gothic rib-vaulted roof is
supported by a central row of columns,
which culminate in a beautiful palm-tree like
semi-circular apse end.

18 Vendome Cathedral, 1300
This small flamboyant Gothic structure has
flame-shaped window tracery and wide
span flying buttresses.

19 Amboise
Seen from the high platform surrounding
the chateau overlooking the Loire River. The
consistent roof slopes covered in grey slate
creates a serene, consistent townscape.

20

22

23

24

20 Rocamadour Accrochée
Clinging dramatically to the cliffs of a river gorge, the stepped and ramped streets offer charming internal spaces and outward views of the Dordogne Valley.

21, 22 Saint-Cirq Lapopie
A charming country townscape with medieval timber framed and brick-infilled houses.

23 Grosbois Chateau, 1580
A typical formally planned steep roofed structure.

24, 25 Langeais Chateau, 1460
The interiors have exposed materials; masonry walls, timber ceilings and glazed tile floors. Tapestries lent warmth to the otherwise hard surfaced spaced.

26 Azay-le-Rideau Chateau, 1520
One of the most exquisite chateaus in the Valley of the Indre River. The nearest thing to a fairy tale castle is surrounded by water and superb forests.

27 Chenonceau, Chateau, 1540
Built across the river, this elegant building with long galleries overlooking the tranquil water has a long history of jealousies of different Kings, their wives and mistresses.

28 Vaux-le-Viconte Chateau, 1660
Architects: Le Veau, Le Notre and Lebrun
The most elegant and grandiose of chateaus and formal gardens. Its owner, Fouquet, was put in jail for daring to outdo the King with such a sumptuous establishment.

29 Chambord, Chateau, start of construction 1590
Architect: Domenico da Cortona
Of all the 16th Century chateaus, this must be the most unbelievably bizarre, bristling with gables, pinnacles, domes and decorated chimneys surrounding a long turreted structure. Its ingenious central double spiral staircase allows a person walking up not to be seen by someone descending.

25

26

27

30

31

30 Valençay, Chateau, 1540
Set in an extensive property with a deer park surrounding the chateau, unusual corner domes give the building a distinctive silhouette.

31, 33 Chantilly, Chateau, 1560
Architect: Bullant
Set in a lake, every façade of the building is of different design and yet achieves cohesion of the whole.

32 Blois, Chateau, 1520-1630
Architect: Mansart
The distinctive element is the polygonal open staircase tower, which offers changing spatial through-views into the courtyard as one ascends.

34 d'Anet Chateau, 1550
Architect: Philibert de l'Orme
Has a fine curvilinear entrance staircase in one of the few remaining parts of the building.

35 Cheverny, Chateau, 1634
Architect: Hurault
Axially approached, the symmetrical building's flat façade achieves distinction from its varying height and shape roof forms. One of the most elegant chateaus in France.

36 Paris, Place des Vosges, 1605-12
Architect: Louis Metezeau
A fine urban square surrounded by arcaded individual residential buildings, each with its own roof. The two larger axial pavilions are reserved for the King and Queen.

32

33

34

35

37 Ménars Chateau, 1760
Architect: Ange-Jacques Gabriel
The formality of the approach is recalled in the artificially trimmed trees.

38, 39 Champs-sur-Seine, Chateau
A formal building with a seemingly endless axially landscaped park on the view side.

40, 42 Versailles Palace 1660
Architects: Le Veau and Mansart
Petit Trianon, 1760, Architect: Gabriel
The most immense palace building in Europe reflecting the total power of Louis XIV. The enormity of the complex is difficult to grasp as is the immense formal land-scaped park and fountains surrounding it. Other than the Hall of Mirrors, it is a complex, less satisfying aesthetically than smaller palaces by the same architects.

41 Maisons–Lafitte Chateau, 1642-48
Architect: François Mansart
An urban grandiose chateau near Paris of majestic scale and great elegance.

43 Versailles Palace
The Hall of Mirrors, by J.H. Mansart Facing the main garden façade. The glittering room seen during a formal occasion.

37

38

39

40

41

42

44

45

44 Paris, The Invalides, 1678-91
Architect: Libéral Bruant
With a 200 metre long façade is one of Paris' landmarks. The building was used as a soldiers' hospital under Napoleon I who is buried in the domed structure at the rear.

45 Paris, Saint-Étienne-du-Mont, start of construction 1592
by Philibert de L'Orme
With its unique screen structure in front of the apse end, spanning between two spiral stone stairs.

46 Paris, Eiffel Tower, 1889
Built for the universal exhibition, this daringly light steel structure has become the iconic landmark of Paris. It is symbolic of new methods of construction.

47 Paris, Place de la Concorde, 1750
Architect: Ange-Jacques Gabriel
This axially placed open urban space, the very centre of Paris, is marked by a granite Egyptian obelisk (see Egypt photo 12 for its pair).

48

49

50

48 Monte Carlo, Casino, 1863
Architect: Charles Garnier
Symbolic of luxurious buildings in Europe's gambling capital.

49 Paris, Opera House, 1861-74
Architect: Charles Garnier
Built in the final phase of romantic 19th Century architecture, it is the ultimate example of decorative classicism.
A sumptuously curved grand staircase joins the high spaces of the foyer. A monument to the architect is built along one exterior façade.

50, 51 Paris, Rue de Rivoli, 1840
by Percier & Fontaine
This one-sided arcaded straight line row of buildings was first built by Napoleon I. Overlooking the Tuileries Gardens, it forms a monumental element in the planning of Paris.

51

52 Menier Chocolate Works, Noisiel-sur-Marne, 1879
Architect: Jules Saulnier
The first iron skeleton supported building with non-structural brick infill exterior walls.

53 Paris, Library Sainte-Geneviève, 1850
Architect: Henri Labrouste
An early expressive wrought and cast iron vaulted structure.

54 Paris, National Library, 1860
Architect: Henri Labrouste
The spherical roof vaults, each with a sky-light, are supported by slim cast iron columns.

55 Paris, Ave Rapp Apartments, 1900
Architect: Jules Lavirotte
A typical art nouveau decorated exterior.

53

54

55

56

56, 59 Paris, Grand Palais, 1897-1900
Architect: Frantz Jourdain
The huge exhibition building supports
its glass dome roof with iron ribs using
inappropriate forms of traditional
masonry vaults.

57, 60, 61 Paris, Métropolitain Stations, 1900
Architect: Hector Guimard
Art Nouveau cast iron and glass structures
in organic decorative forms.

58 Paris, Rue Reaumur, 1900
Architect: Georges Chedanne
An early example of exposed steel framed
construction.

58

59

60

61

156

62 Paris, Rue Franklin, 1903
Architect: August Perret
Concrete framed, glass infilled apartment building.

63 Paris
Roofscape in the Left-Bank District with skylight artists' ateliers.

64 Paris, Place Vendôme, 1700
Architect: J.H. Mansart
A monumental octagonal urban space with a metal clad sculpted central stone column. Luxurious shops and apartments surround the space.

65 Paris, La Défense, 1970's
This new expansion area of the city was planned to house skyscraper offices and apartments with public transport and garages below the "Grand Axe", a kilometres long extension ending in the "Grande Arche" building from the Louvre through the "Arc de Triumphe", along one of Paris' main axis. The vast public plaza houses sculptures by Calder, Miro, etc.

62

63

64

65

66

66, 67 Villa Garches, 1927
Architect: Le Corbusier
This luxurious house built for the famous Stein family in the country near Paris represents an important milestone in Le Corbusier's work. It demonstrates the clear separation of structure and infill, enabling spaces to be free and open aesthetically, both horizontally and vertically. This seminal building has influenced architecture to this day.

68

68-70 Paris, Villa La Roche-Jeanneret, 1923
Architect: Le Corbusier
An early duplex residence with interiors of spatial complexity. The building now houses the Le Corbusier Foundation.

71-72 Paris, Apartments, 1933
Architect: Le Corbusier
The glass and glass blocks curtain wall building houses the architect's two-storey penthouse and landscaped roof terrace.

69

73 Paris, Swiss Students Pavilion, University of Paris, 1930
Architect: Le Corbusier
Supported on central concrete pylons and a steel superstructure, all students' rooms have straight south facing glass walls, contrasted by the sculptural forms of the common room and vertical core.

74-77 Poissy, Villa Savoie, 1929
Architect: Le Corbusier
The iconic best known of the architect's houses, is built on a large property outside of Paris. The dramatic spatial fusion of the upper level hollow centre with access ramps and spiral stairs make this a supreme example of the fusion of art and architecture.

70

71

72

73

78 Paris, Salvation Army Refuge, 1929
Architect: Le Corbusier
An early framed structure and the first
totally sealed air conditioned glass curtain
wall building. The façade was altered after
World War II.

**79,81 Marseille, L'Unité d'habitation
1947**
Architect: Le Corbusier
The tower contains split-level apartments
with a central shopping floor, a roof top
kindergarten and communal facilities.

80 Le Corbusier 1887-1965

82-89 The Chapel at Ronchamp, 1950
Architect: Le Corbusier
This represents a unique sculptural
departure from conventional modern architecture. The awe-inspiring curvilinear interior
receives daylight from various apertures in
side-walls and top light through attached
tower structures. The huge pivoted entrance
is covered with a colourful metal mural by
the architect.

78

79

82

83

84

**aris, Brazilian Students'
iversity of Paris, 1957**
Corbusier

s' room faces a sunny
ground level adjuncts contain
cilities and a separate wing of
residence.

nvent of La Tourette, 1960
Corbusier

ntral courtyard is surrounded
oms and communal facilities.
ırful chapel is adjacent to the
hall.

plex Jaoul Residence, 1956
Corbusier

ls and off form concrete
structure's colourful interiors
orned.

90

91

93

100-106 Paris, UNESCO Headquarters
1953
Architect: Marcel Breuer
The three curved office wings, supported
by tapered columns, are connected to the
large assembly hall with a folded concrete
structure by the engineer Pier Luigi Nervi.
Artworks throughout the complex are by
Arp, Calter, Miro, Moore and Picasso.

107 Paris, The Pyramid in the Louvre
1981
Architect: Ieoh Ming Pei
The ephemeral transparent pyramid is
placed over the large entry space leading
down to the wings of the museum.

101

102

103

104

105

106

United Kingdom

The peak achievement in historic English architecture are the great number of churches and cathedrals built in the Gothic era. Medieval villages still maintain their unique charm, as does the elegant restraint of the numerous country manors and universities built in the Renaissance and Baroque periods.

Rather than the grandiose formal axes of French urban developments, the architecture of English cities is on a smaller scale and gains from the interaction of diverse styles side-by-side, often built centuries apart.

The building of continuous long terrace house developments in the 18th and 19th Century gives its own grandeur on smaller scale to towns, culminating in the superb urban planning of cities like Bath, which has been meticulously maintained and remains as valid today as it was 250 years ago.

The Industrial Revolution, technological and scientific advances were dramatic in the 19th Century, which brought a new vision to English architecture. Building upon 18th Century inventions of the use of iron in construction, the (later) glass and iron exhibition buildings influenced the rest of Europe.

The development of modern architecture aesthetically did not gain a foothold in England until just before World War II, with only a few distinguished buildings remaining. Although leaders of the modern movement in Europe (Gropius, Breuer, Mendelsohn, etc) came to England in the 1930's, having left Germany due to its emerging fascism, they were not welcomed professionally and left to teach and practice successfully in the USA.

Advances in building technology took a leap forward after the war with the work of outstandingly inventive architects, now leading the way internationally.

1 Bath, Prior Park, 1755
Architect: John Wood Snr
This fine property and bridge were developed by the architect. The landscape architecture was done by Capability Brown.

2

2 Norwich, Elm Hill
A charming, well preserved medieval
cobble stoned street.

**3 Norwich, Cathedral, 11th-14th
Century**
One of the finest of early English Gothic.

4

5

6

4 Dorset, Shaftsbury, Gold Hill
With its thatched roofs, is a favourite
film location.

5, 6 Salisbury, Cathedral, 1220-56
Considered the purest of English Gothic
architecture cohesive in style, as it was built
in a short time.

**7 Cambridge, Kings College Chapel,
1512-15**
The perpendicular Gothic fan vaulting was
designed by John Wastell.

**8 Gloucester, Cathedral Cloister,
1360-nearly 1400**
Early experimental fan vaulting.

7

8

9

10

9 Ely, Cathedral Octagon, 14th Century
The central tower collapsed and was
replaced by the timber framed lantern.

**10 Ely, Cathedral Lady Chapel,
15th Century**
Vaulting.

11 London, Westminster Abbey, 1245

12

13

14

**12,13 East Anglia, Blickling Hall,
16th Century**
A Jacobean country house, the one time
home of Anne Boleyn, mother of Elizabeth I.

**14 Scotland, Drumlanrig Castle,
1679-1691**
Distinguished by Baroque horseshoe-
shaped entrance stairs and multiple towers.

15

15 London, Chiswick House, 1725
Architect: Lord Burlington
Country house with perfect ancient Roman and Palladian elements. The focal space is an octagonal domed salon.

16 London, Greenwich, The Grand Hall, 1700
Architect: Christopher Wren

17 London, Greenwich, The Royal Naval College by Christopher Wren with the Queens House beyond by Inigo Jones, 1620.

18 London, Horse Guard, 1755
Architect: William Kent

16

23

24

19 Oxford, Christ Church Cathedral, 1160

20 Oxford, Radcliffe Camera, 1750
Architect: James Gibbs

21 Oxford, Christ Church Tom Tower, 1681
Architect: Christopher Wren

22 Oxford, Queen's College

23, 24 Bath, Prior Park, 1834
Architect: Henry Edmund Goodridge
A curved and counter-curved stair leading up to the main wing, now used as a school

25 Bath, Lansdowne Crescent, 1790
A continuous wave-shaped line of housing overlooking a valley.

26 Bath, The Circus, 1705-54
Architect: John Wood the elder

27, 28 Bath, The Royal Crescent, 1767
Architect: John Wood the younger
This grandiose town planning assembly of geometric building forms gives an unprecedented cohesive character to the whole town. The housing was built by the Woods, as commercial development.

5

6

27

28

29

31

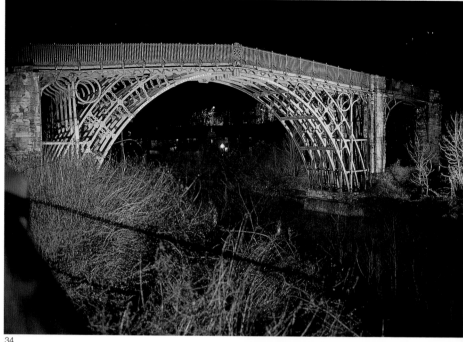

34

29 London, Carlton House Terrace, The Mall, 1827-33
Architect: John Nash
These formal Classic Buildings form the boulevard leading to Buckingham Palace.

30 London, Regents Park Crescent, 1812
Architect: John Nash
Two colonnaded arc forms face Regents Park, becoming one of the grandest Terrace development of joined houses.

31 London, Pelham Crescent, 1840
Architect: George Basevi

32 London, Royal Opera Arcade, 1818
Architect: John Nash
Strong co-ordinated architectural forms and cohesive timber shop fronts are beautifully maintained.

33 London, Burlington Arcade, 1820
Architect: Samuel Ware
Small finely detailed shops with a glass roof have remained popular for nearly 200 years.

35

34, 35 Ironbridge, 1779
Engineer: Abraham Darby
The world's first iron bridge, which
revolutionised building methods.

36 Glasgow
Unified 19th Century, masonry row
housing and bay windowed glass fronts.

**37 The Glasgow School of Arts,
1897-1909**
Architect: Charles Rennie Mackintosh
The library demonstrates the new spatial
design by the architect, who influenced
pioneering Viennese architecture at the
time.

36

37

38

39

40

38, 40 Brighton, The Royal Pavilion, 1820
Architect: John Nash
This orientally decorated building and its structure, seen in the kitchen, is characteristic of the Prince Regent's exotic taste.

39 Brighton, The Palace Pier, 1899
The focal point of this seaside resort.

41 Brighton
Typical Georgian residence influential to colonial architecture in the 19th Century.

41

42

4

15

16

47

42 London, Bedford Square, 1775
Architect: Thomas Leverton
The four facades of the Square's sides face an exclusive private central park space.

43 London, Regent Street, 1820
Architect: John Nash
The gracefully curved huge classic facades have become one of the main shopping areas.

44 London Zoo, Penguin Pool, 1934
Architect: Berthold Lubetkin and Tecton
An imaginative early use of thin reinforced concrete curved slabs creates a sculptural totality.

45 Bexhill, De La Warr Pavilion, 1935
Architects: Mendelsohn and Chermayeff
The community building is a rare early example of distinguished modern architecture in England.

46 Cambridge, Gonville & Caius College, 1960
Architects: Leslie Martin & Colin St. John Wilson

47 University of East Anglia, 1962
Architect: Denys Lasdun
Stepped terraces of student accommodation in irregularly sited buildings face the riverside views.

48 London, Roehampton L.C.C. Housing, 1955
Architect: Robert Matthew
Facing Richmond Park, this development constitutes an exemplary high point of English public housing.

49

49, 51, 52 Norwich, Sainsbury Centre, 1978
Architect: Norman Foster
A technologically advanced structure with co-ordinated solid and glazed components.

50, 53 London, Canary Wharf Station 1995
Architect: Norman Foster
A monumentally scaled underground station of structurally expressive concrete.

54 Stansted Airport, 1989
Architect: Norman Foster
A rare refined example of airport architecture, free of normal visual confusion and clutter, with all services and signage co-ordinated within the inverted pyramidal shaped sky-lit steel supports.

55 London, British Museum, 2000
Architect: Norman Foster
The courtyard's flat glazed dome inventively uses glass as a structural compressive element.

51

52

53

54

57

56, 57 London, Lloyd's Insurance Headquarters, 1982
Architect: Richard Rogers
An important building of advanced technology with expressed structure and mechanical services.

58 London, The Eye, 1999
Architects: Marks Barfield Architects
The gigantic steel Ferris wheel with its moving cabins is structurally inventive and offers panoramic views over the Thames and the city.

Spain

Spain has had an extraordinary history, varied with cultural extremes of opposites. The Romans named the land Iberia or Hispania and built roads, bridges and huge engineering works such as the stone aqueduct in Segovia, which still serves its purpose after 2000 years. Invasions by the Moors from North Africa brought other than European architecture, which thrived for centuries and stood side by side with fine late Gothic structures such as in Seville and Córdoba. The pleasure pavilions in Granada's Alhambra became the most celebrated pieces of architecture in Spain. During the cruel, autocratic reign of Philip II in the 16th Century, vast Monasteries were built of solid granite - such as "Escorial", by virtual slave labour, many of whom died on the building site.

The cities of Spain are graced with wonderful, huge public plazas - ringed with four sides of co-ordinated buildings. They were built in the 17th and 18th Centuries and remain the popular focus of their towns.

The most extraordinary Catalan architect, nearer our time, was Antoní Gaudí. He designed the church La Sagrada Família in 1883, which is still in construction long after his death. His intuitive structures are embellished within curvilinear forms, which characterise all his work.

During the Civil War and in the fascist Franco period, many architects and artist (such as Picasso) chose to live outside Spain. There are few modern buildings of distinction of that period.

1 Barcelona, Casa Milà, 1906-10
Architect: Antoní Gaudí
Detail of Façade

1

3

2 Barcelona
The Gothic quarter of Barcelona dates back to Roman times, although built in the 13th-15th Centuries.

3 Barcelona
The 15th Century Gothic Cathedral is. originally of French design, reconstructed in the 19th Century.

4, 6 Barcelona, La Sagrada Família, 1883 - still in construction
Architect: Antoní Gaudí
This building is the landmark of Barcelona. Long after Gaudí's death the interior structure is finally being completed following the original design but executed in part using pre-cast concrete instead of stone.

5 Barcelona, La Sagrada Família, 1883 - still in construction
Architect: Antoní Gaudí
In spite of its fanciful appearance, it contains rational structural expressions in its column form, predating the work of Piere Luigi Nervi.

7 Barcelona, Casa Milà, 1906-10
Architect: Antoní Gaudí
The unique undulating façade and rooftop sculptural chimneys, this apartment building's character is extended to every detail of the interior.

4

5

8 Barcelona, Casa Batlló, 1904
Architect: Antoní Gaudí
The curvilinear stone façade recalls organic forms.

9 Barcelona, Güell Pavilion, 1885
Architect: Antoní Gaudí
Iron fence.

10, 11 Barcelona, Casa Milà, 1906-10
Architect: Antoní Gaudí
The main entrance doors handmade of beaten wrought iron.

12 Barcelona, Casa Milà, 1906-10
Architect: Antoní Gaudí
The rooftops sculptural chimneys.

13 Montefrío

14 Toledo

15 Setenil

16 Olvera
Southern Spain's characteristic white hill towns gain visual consistency using white painted walls and terracotta roofs for all buildings old and new.

17 Castille
Isolated fortified medieval castle in the Castille area.

9

10

11

12

13

9

0

18-21 El Escorial Monastery, 1563
Architect: Juan de Herrera
The sober clean-cut lines of this majestic Monument belie its age. Built entirely of grey granite it achieves the grandeur of a palace and the austerity of a monastery.

1

22-24 Segovia, Cathedral, 16th Century
Architect: Juan Gil de Hontañón
A fine late Gothic work.

25 Segovia, Roman Aqueduct
This daring 28 m high structure (1st Century AD) still serves its purpose as an aqueduct.

26, 27 Ronda
This Roman town is built on a platform at the edge of a ravine. It contains the oldest bullring in Spain.

22

23

24

25

29

28, 29 Córdoba
For centuries the centre of Muslim Spain.
The huge arched mosque structure, 875-
987 AD, had a Christian Cathedral inserted
n its centre in the 16th Century.

30 Córdoba
The 13th Century interlocking cross vaults
are reminiscent of Guarino Guarini's work in
17th Century Turin.

230

31 Granada, Cathedral façade
17th Century
Architect: Alonso Cano
Seen during a historic celebration.

32-35 Granada, The Alhambra, 1350
An elaborate and richly decorated Muslim fortress palace with formal pavilions; the lion court and the arcaded Myrtles court with a central reflecting pool.

31

32

3

4

36

37

36, 37 Granada, Palace of Charles V, in the Alhambra, 1550
Architect: Pedro & Luis Machuca
A square Renaissance building, with an internal arcaded circular court.

38 Burgos, Town Gate
14th Century

39, 40 Madrid, Plaza Mayor, 1620
Architect: Juan Gomez de Mora
This public square surrounded by fine buildings, forms the focus of Habsburg Madrid, used for celebrations.

38

39

41 Burgos, Cathedral, 1490
Architect: Simon de Colonia
The octagonal Chapel Contestable.

42 Burgos, Cathedral
Sculptured Coroneria doorway.

43 Salamanca, Plaza Mayor, 1730
Architect: Churriguera Bros
One of the finest squares in Spain much frequented by University students.

44

45

46

47

48

49

44 Salamanca, University, 1520
Sculpted entrance façade.

45-47 Salamanca, New Cathedral, Started 1513
Architect: Juan Gil de Hontanon
The decorative fan vaulting extends into the transept.

48, 49 Ávila
This picturesque, intact, fortified 11th Century town has accessible continuous ramparts.

50-53 Barcelona, German Pavilion, 1929
Architect: Ludwig Mies van der Rohe
This ultimate icon of modern architecture was erected for the International exhibition in 1929, demolished after a mere three months and faithfully reconstructed permanently as a museum in 1986.
The concentration of support in regularly placed steel columns allowed the free disposition, independently, of screen-like walls that create a continuum of flowing space between them.
This spatial openness is dramatised by the use of the most sumptuous materials, polished marble, onyx, travertine and polished chrome. Two reflecting pools complete this dramatic demonstration of the new language in architecture, amplified by the architect's specially designed chairs, which have become famous internationally. There are no exhibits in the building, which in itself serves that purpose. The black carpet, yellow leather upholstery on the chairs and a red curtain, the colours of the German flag, confirm this.

50

51

52

54

55

56

57

54, 56, 57 Bilbao, Underground Station, 1991
Architect: Norman Foster
Approached through glass arched entries from street level, the upper station concourse is suspended from the wide precast concrete vaulted station roof.

55 Barcelona, Miró Foundation, 1976
Architect: José Luis Sert
The museum is dedicated to Sert's friend and countryman, the Spanish artist Miró. The various pavilions showing different phases of Miró's work are top lit from segmental concrete vaults, which throw diffused daylight onto the artworks and create a rich spaciousness within.

58 Bilbao, Footbridge, 1997
Engineer: Santiago Calatrava
This extraordinary structure has the translucent glass walkway (dramatically lit from within at night) suspended from a one-sided tilting arch support.

58

60

59-61 Bilbao, Guggenheim Museum, 1997

Architect: Frank Gehry

This amazing unprecedented sculptural building is made possible in our computer era which not only enables architects to draw such designs accurately, but by the computer instructing machines to produce all elements for assembly. There are virtually no straight or perpendicular lines in the building. The exterior is sheathed with panels of Titanium.

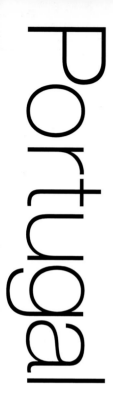

Portugal

Even though Portugal has some of the richest examples of Gothic and Baroque Building Art, their importance and historic value have largely gone unnoticed. It seems that historians did not visit Portugal and have always concentrated on other centres of European architectural culture.
The country's rich background dates from the golden age of Portuguese discoveries when its navigators set sail to explore the New World. This gained its huge wealth from trade in spices from the East and gold and sugar from plantations in colonial Brazil. The wealth made possible the many distinctive, well preserved monuments.
Due to the country's warm and sunny climate, central European architectural styles through the ages were transformed into more open and different configurations.
A traditional craft, the production of fine blue "Azulejos" wall tiles used to cover large exterior wall areas, gives a unique character to Portuguese historic buildings.
The Baroque buildings of the 17th and 18th Centuries, in comparison to those of central Europe, create an extraordinary flamboyant sculptural imagery, which find their parallels in the historic towns of Brazil.

Tomar, Azulejos Wall

Batalha, Cloister, 1500

3

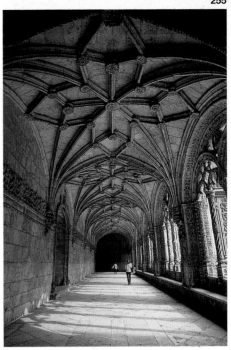

4

3, 4 Belém, Monastery of Jeronimos, 1495-1521

Architect: Diogo de Boytac

An example of Manueline Architecture with distinctive rib vaulting and cloisters.

5

5 Vila Viçosa, "Knot Gate", 16th Centur
Entry carved of solid stone.

6 Lisbon, Terreiro do Paço, 18th Centur
The finest square in Lisbon with a statue
of King Carlos I and a monumental arch
leading into the city.

7 Lisbon, Santa Justa Lift Tower, 1898-1901
Constructed by the French Engineer Gustav
Eiffel.

8 Lisbon, Monument to the Discoveries 1960
by Padrao dos Descobrimentos
To mark the 500th anniversary of Prince
Henry, the Navigator, shown pointing
the way.

9-12 Tomar, Church of Nossa Senhora, 12th Century
With an intricately carved façade, ribbed
vaulting, curved stone stairs and Azulejo
tiled cloistered courtyards.

13 Coimbra, 18th Century
University entrance portico leading to the
ceremonial Hall and a fine 17th Century
Manueline chapel by Marcos Pires decorated
with Azulejos.

7

8

11

14

14 Coimbra, 18th Century
University entrance portico leading to the
ceremonial Hall and a fine 17th Century
Manueline chapel by Marcos Pires decorate
with Azulejos.

15, 17 Batalha, Santa Maria da Vitória
The late 14th Century monastery and
church built by an Irishman in flamboyant
Gothic style for the English Queen Philippa
of Lancaster. The Royal Cloister is
surrounded by carved marble arcades.

**16 Coimbra, Monastery of the Holy
Cross, 16th Century**
With a freestanding Renaissance portico.

15

16

17

18

8 Óbidos Castle
The medieval building was transformed into a palace in the 16th Century, built against the old town wall.

9 Porto
A huge Azulejos tiled exterior church wall.

0 Buçaco Forest
Fed by a natural spring, the "Cold Fountain", flanked by staircases on both sides, cascades down in the magnificent forest.

1 Porto, Dom Luis I Bridge, 1886
Engineer: Theophile Seyrig
This iron engineering feat has two superimposed roads, connecting both upper and lower levels of the town on either side of the river.

2 Braga, Bom Jesus do Monte
Architect: Carlos Amarante
The twin towered 18th Century pilgrimage church stands atop a granite and plaster Baroque staircase, adorned with fountains and terracotta statues. The form of this long double stair built into the natural hillside is one of the richest examples of Baroque art.

20

21

Netherlands

To most visitors, the cities of Netherlands especially Amsterdam, conjure up the image of tree lined canals with charming narrow fronted row houses on both sides; hence the name "The Venice of the North". Although this ubiquitous historic character is typical, the emergence of the Architectural "Amsterdam School" at the beginning of the 20th Century is prevalent in more recent buildings. It is a solid style of socially "comfortable" buildings with a few individual architects raising it to architectural importance. The best known of these is Hendrik Berlage, the architect of the Amsterdam Stock Exchange, which is a powerful large building of brick, inside and out, of visible structural expression and no applied decoration. The few carved embellishments are set into the fabric of the building to form an integral part of it.

In the 1920's and 30's, the "De Stijl" movement, both in painting and architecture, produced some buildings of world importance, which influenced architecture in the rest of the western world, even to this day. Aside from Dutch artists such as Piet Mondrian and Theo van Doesburg, a revolutionary small house and its furniture designed by Gerrit Rietveld in Utrecht, and the work of Jacobus Johannes Pieter Oud have influenced modern building throughout the country.

Developing in parallel with the new art and architecture at the Bauhaus in Germany, some large pioneering buildings stand out as landmark structures which are now as valid visually and physically as they were in the 1920's such as the famous van Nelle factory in Rotterdam by Brinkman and van der Vlugt, or the Bergpolder, Gallery-Access Apartments by Willem van Tijen.

1

1 Rotterdam, van Nelle Factory, 1924
Architects: Brinkman & van der Vlugt
One of the earliest total glass curtain wall
buildings in Europe expressly designed for
the comfort and safety of employees.

2 Amsterdam
Typical tree lined canal with joined buildings
on both sides.

272

3

3 Amsterdam, Open Air School, 1930
Architect: Johannes Duiker
An early reinforced concrete glazed
structure with cantilevered corners. The
building is as new, still used for its original
purpose.

4 Amsterdam
Narrow fronted buildings along canals with
characteristically Dutch gables, large
windows and lifting beams projecting from
the roof to raise furniture.

5 Amsterdam
Typical tree lined canal with joined buildings
on both sides.

6 Amsterdam, Stock Exchange, 1903
Architect: Hendrik Petrus Berlage
An early minimalist structurally expressive
brick building.

5

6

8

7, 8 Utrecht, Schröder House, 1924
Architect: Gerrit Rietveld
The most famous of "De Stijl" buildings with a flexible subdividable open interior is a publicly accessible museum.
Opposing vertical and horizontal slab-like walls and continuous glass areas create compositions with their "tensional" window sub-divisions recall the work of Dutch artists at the time.

9 Amsterdam
The tranquility and charm of a typical Dutch town's canal.

Belgium

This small multilingual country can boast a
fine, exceptionally tall, Gothic Cathedral in
Antwerp and the 17th Century Guild House
ringing Brussels' Grand Place, as its historic heritage. The Guild Houses have richly
decorated gabled facades, some adorned
with gold leaf, between their large window
The facades are all different and yet form a
unified totality in this focal point of Brussel
The unique architectural development, how
ever, emerged at the turn of the 19th and
early 20th Centuries in the work of Victor
Horta, exemplified in his own house, which
is now a public museum. His work is a rare
combination of flamboyant "Art Nouveau"
linear decoration (such as on stair railings
and lamp posts), with deliberately exposed
iron structural elements, columns and gird-
ers. These proudly show the pattern of the
riveted connections, all intertwined with
the swirling curvilinear patterns of Horta's
special kind of strap iron ornamentation.
The strength of this work is based on the
contrast of plain wall surfaces of stone, tile
or brick, with the unrolled curls and rosette
of his linear metal embellishments.
Beyond the materials and the decorative
combinations they are given, it is the new
Space Horta creates in his buildings that
particularly herald the future.
In his own house the central stair gives
access to open split-level arrangements of
rooms leading from it. This allows for continuous spaciousness to emerge, even in
the limited size of his buildings. Such fusing
of levels and spaces became the hallmark
of modern architecture more than two
decades later.

1 Brussels, Solvay House, 1896
Architect: Victor Horta
The polished stone stair and walls are
combined with characteristic flat iron
ornate railing. They are in contrast to the
exposed riveted steel columns and beams

2

4

2-4 Brussels, Horta House, 1898
Architect: Victor Horta
The central curved stair with flat iron
decoration, gives access to split-level
floors, creating a continuity of spatial
effects. Walls are of bare glazed brick
and tiles reaching the top floor with a
curved glass skylight.

5

5 Brussels, 17th Century
Guild Houses ringing the Grand Place with
gold leaf decoration between large windows.

6 Antwerp
Gothic Cathedral with its central tall tower.

7 Antwerp
The town square with touching
gabled facades.

Denmark

Denmark's architecture is related to that of
other Scandinavian countries. The richly
decorated gables of historic structures are
punctuated by high spires, the most famous being Copenhagen's 16th Century
stock exchange's spiral tower.
The country has consistently produced excellent modern buildings, particularly by the
architect Arne Jacobson, whose furniture
and the design of objects of use are known
worldwide.
The most brilliant of Danish architects how
ever, is Jørn Utzon, who won the international competition for the Sydney Opera
House, which has become the very icon of
Australia. After leaving that project, due to
controversy prior to its completion, he pro-
ceeded to create some wonderful buildings
and furniture elsewhere. One of the finest is
the Bagsvaerd Church and the exemplary
Fredensborg group housing near Copenhagen. It showed the practical and aesthet
ic advantages of such housing rather than
routine suburbia.

1,3 Copenhagen, Nyhavn
The picturesque canal dating from the 17th
Century, which has become a popular pe-
destrian promenade and boat anchorage.

2 Copenhagen
The charming central pedestrian district.

4

6

7

4-7 Copenhagen, Bagsvaerd Church, 1976

Architect: Jørn Utzon
One of the finest works of Utzon after leaving the Sydney Opera House project. The wave-like form of the interior is surrounded by a stepped rectilinear structure, and enclosed courts that create a unique dichotomy of spaces.

8 Copenhagen, Amalienborg Palace, 1750

Architect: Nils Eigtved
An assembly of restrained classic structures forming an octagonal public space.

Finland

Formerly part of Sweden, Finland became
an autonomous part of Russia and Helsinki
its capital. The new Neo-Classical centre
was built largely by the German architect
Carl Engel, the focal point of which is the
hilltop Lutheran Cathedral of 1830. Its spar
kling white and gilded exterior still dominates the city.
The design competition for the Central
Railway Terminal was won in 1904 by Eliel
Saarinen (the father of Eero Saarinen who
later produced some fine architecture in the
USA). The building, completed in 1914,
shows Art Nouveau stylistic influences,
which dominated whole districts of Helsinki
As in many of his other buildings, the use
of solid granite exteriors has made it remair
in pristine condition for nearly a century.
Geographically isolated from the rest of
Europe, Finland was late to be industri-
alised. It maintained its handicraft traditions
until the 1920's, which gave rise to the
creation of the finest modern design products in the world today; textiles, glass-
ware, crockery, cutlery, furniture, etc.
The leading figure in Finnish architecture
and furniture design was Alvar Aalto who
influenced a whole generation of modern
architects world wide, evidenced by the
high standard of design and town planning
in the country.

1 Tapiola
Typical groups of apartments set in un-
touched pine tree forests and granite out-
crops.

2 Helsinki, Lutheran Cathedral, 1830-52
Architect: Carl Engel
The glistening white classic building stands
on a commanding hilltop.

4

3 Helsinki, Central Railway Terminal, 1910
Architect: Eliel Saarinen
The solid granite building with Art Nouveau sculptures and decoration.

4 Helsinki, National Museum, 1902-10
Architect: Eliel Saarinen
Has a finely carved granite façade, especially a bear, which is a Finnish symbol.

300

5

6

5, 6 Paimio, Sanatorium, 1929-33
Architect: Alvar Aalto
Standing in a remote forest of tall pine trees, this present day fully functioning pristine white building complex, belies its age inside and out. The interiors are cheerfully bright and colourful.

7 Helsinki Olympic Stadium Tower, 194
Architects: Yrjö Lindegren & Toivo Jäntti
The 72 m high elegantly slim concrete outlook tower was completed for the 1940 Olympic Games, which due to the war were not held there until 1952.

8

8-10 Helsinki, Finlandia Hall, open 1971
Architect: Alvar Aalto
Beautifully sited along a water frontage, the
long building is surrounded by a park. The
white marble clad exterior is in contrast to
the warm tones of the interior. Round dark
blue wall tiles are used to protect heavily
trafficked areas.

9

10

11

11 Tapiola Centre

Community buildings, a church, the Espoo cultural centre (Architect Arto Sipinen, 1989), a public pool, etc, are built around a lake, which had been an unused brick pit. In my view, the environment created in the totally planned new town of Tapiola achieves the highest physical standard for civilised life, anywhere in today's world.

2

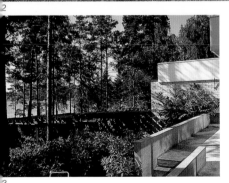

3

12, 13 Tapiola, 1950's
Planner/Architect: Arne Ervi
This Garden City, set in natural surroundings, is an extension area 10 km from Helsinki. It contains a variety of courtyard houses, spaciously placed waterfront townhouses and apartment blocks.

14 Helsinki University of Technology, Otaniemi, 1966
Architect: Alvar Aalto
This large quadrant shaped building contains three lecture halls with steeply rising seating.

Austria

As I was born in Vienna and lived there until the age of 15, I feel a particular affinity with the City, which I grew to love as much as the spectacular mountain scenery in the countryside of Austria.

Vienna has a long and dramatic history. It started as the town Vindobona in Roman times and centuries later developed into the capital of a large empire that covered much of Europe, from the Veneto to the border with Russia until its dismemberment into a small country after World War I.

What is left to us of Vienna, the capital of a once wealthy empire, is a city serving a small country with the heritage of extravagant palaces and churches.

Massive Gothic Cathedrals and Monasteries were built in the 12th and 13th Century with beautifully rib-vaulted naves and equal height aisles, and also the distinctively picturesque onion-domed towers of village churches throughout the mountainous provinces.

A great building boom started in the period of peace following the defeat of the Turkish armies in 1683 that had laid siege to Vienna.

Surrounding the "Hofburg", the seat of the Hapsburg Rulers, palaces were built by the Nobles throughout the medieval city centre which was surrounded by high fortification walls. In this, during the 18th Century high Baroque period, elaborate churches and ambitious establishments of the aristocracy came into being. The celebrated architects of the time, such as Fischer von Erlach and Lucas von Hildebrandt are responsible for the Spanish Riding School, the National Library, the Schönbrum summer palace, etc.

In mid 19th Century the wall surrounding the city was razed and a wide boulevard, the "Ringstrasse" took its place, lined with sumptuous civic buildings; the Parliament, the famous Opera House, museums (housing the Habsburg art collection), the City Hall, theatres, the University, etc.

At the turn of the 20th Century, the ferment of feverish artistic activity created a reaction against conservative Classicism in the arts particularly in architecture, symbolised by the Sezession movement and its exhibition uilding's famous inscription "To each era s art and to art its freedom". With this redo, the foundations of modern architecure were laid by such luminaries as Otto Vagner, Adolf Loos and Josef Hoffmann. ollowing the First World War, to alleviate he dreadful housing conditions, the newly roclaimed republic dedicated itself to the uilding of public housing for all. More than alf of Vienna's population now lives in such ousing in exemplary planned areas that to late have no equal in the rest of the ivilised world.

1

1 Krems
The town portal with Medieval and Baroque decorative towers.

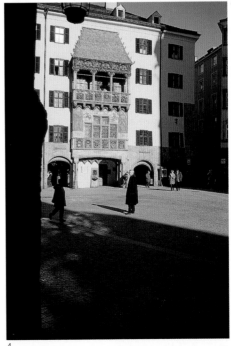

2 Innsbruck, Rococo façade of Helblinghaus

3 Innsbruck

4 Innsbruck, the "Goldenes Dachl", 1500

5 Stams Abbey, 17th Century

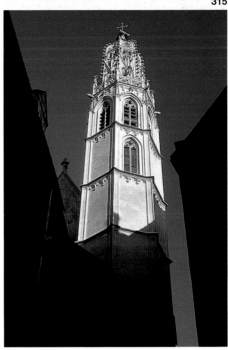

7

6, 7 Maria am Gestade, 15th Century
Structurally expressive ribbed vaulting and
Gothic decorated tower.

8

9

---

8 Wachau Church
Equally high Gothic vaulting over nave and aisles.

9 Salzburg
Gothic vaulting.

10 Dürnstein
The 15th Century church was rebuilt in the Baroque period, standing on the edge of the Donau, below the high up castle where Richard Lionheart was kept prisoner in the 13th Century.

11 Stein
Façade with applied Baroque ornament.

12 Lofer
Picturesque Austrian mountain village with onion domed church tower.

15

13, 14 Vienna, Jesuit Church, 1626-31
The richly gilded interior is crowned by
a Trompe-L'-Oeil dome fresco by
Andrea Pozzo.

15 Vienna, St Peter's Church, 1702-30
Architect: Lucas von Hildebrandt
The exterior with its inward tilted towers
and concave front façade make the
building fit comfortably into the restrictive
site.

7

6 Vienna, St. Stephan's Cathedral
The 14th Century Cathedral stands in an extensive pedestrian precinct. The glazed modern Haas House façade opposite the Cathedral would not be permitted in most cities. It adds to the rich mixture of surrounding important buildings dating from different centuries.

7 Vienna, Spanish Riding School, 18th Century
Architect: Fischer von Erlach
The white colonnaded wide span long hall is home to the unique performances of Lippizaner horses trained to do difficult jumps, steps and dances, all in unison with musical accompaniment.

18

18, 19 Vienna, Piaristen Church, 1700
Architect: Lucas von Hildebrandt
The brilliant Baroque spatial interior has indirect natural light reaching the central nave from hidden overhead sources.

20 Vienna, Karlskirche, 1715
Architect: Fischer von Erlach
This amazing Baroque Church has a classic temple portico flanked by two freestanding minaret-like pylons leading to a high oval domed interior.

21

22

21, 22 Vienna, Liechtenstein Palais, 1700
Architect: Domenico Martinelli
A grand staircase rises to the central hall decorated with a perspective ceiling fresco by Andrea Pozzo.

23 Vienna, Armoury, Am Hof, 1731-32
Architect: Anton Ospel
Originally built as a civil armoury, since 1870 it is used as Vienna's ornate Fire Brigade Headquarters.

24 Melk, Benedictine Monastery, early 18th Century
Architect: Jacob Prandtauer
Dramatically sited on a high rocky ledge above the Danube, the monumental church interior is sumptuously gilded, as is the adjacent library.

25, 26 Vienna, Belvedere Palace, 1721
Architect: Lucas von Hildebrandt
Built for Prince Eugene of Savoy in gratitude after his defeat of the Turks who surrounded the city in 1683. The palace has a commanding view of Vienna over its formal gardens and fountains, which has not changed since Bellotto (called Canaletto) painted the scene in the 18th Century.

27 Vienna, Schönbrunn Summer Palace, 1680-1740
Architects: Fischer von Erlach and Nikolaus Parcassi

28

29

28, 30 Vienna, Schönbrunn Summer Palace, 1680-1740

Architects: Fischer von Erlach and Nikolaus Parcassi

The Empress Maria Theresa was determined to outdo Louis 14th's Palace at Versailles. Even though Schönbrunn is smaller, it has more charm and human scale. The interiors are sumptuously appointed and the axial formal gardens focus on the Gloriette (architect von Hohenberg) built on high ground.

29, 31 Vienna, Schönbrunn Palm House, 1880-1882

Architect: Franz von Segenschmid

30

31

32

33

4

5

32, 33 Vienna, Hofburg Palace
The historic residence of the Emperor was built in many stages from the 15th to the early 20th Century in various wings around formal courts.

34, 35 Vienna, Kinsky Palace, 1713-16
Architect: Lucas von Hildebrandt
The city residence of a Noble has a grand staircase crowned with a fresco by Chiarini.

36

36 Vienna, Pestsäule, 1693
Architect: Fischer von Erlach
Erected on the Graben Plaza to give thanks
at the end of the plague, which had
decimated the population.

37 St. Florian Abbey Library, 1690
Architect: Jacob Prandtauer

38 Hallstadt
Romantically picturesque town on
the edge of a lake at the foothills of the
Dachstein Mountain.

39 Vienna, Kunsthistorisches Museum, 1875

Architect: Karl Hasenauer
The grandiose classic building houses the Habsburg's important and extensive art collection.

40 Vienna, Steinhof Church, 1905-07

Architect: Otto Wagner
Even though the silhouette of the domed church appears classical, the embellishments and especially the interior speak a totally new visual language; white marble, gilding and Secessionist forms.

39

40

41

42

41 Vienna, Ringstrasse
After the demolition of the medieval fortification walls in 1858, the Parliament (1874, architect Theophil Hansen) and other public buildings and parks were built along the resulting wide tree-lined Boulevard.

42 Vienna, Stadtpark
Gilded monument to Johann Strauss.

43

43 Vienna, Postsparkasse, 1906
Architect: Otto Wagner
This most inventive and progressive
building for its time has a glass roofed
banking hall and specially designed air
heating columns, light fixtures and
furniture.
The thick granite exterior facing is secured
with exposed metal bolts.

44 Vienna, Loos Haus, 1910
Architect: Adolf Loos
The first, totally undecorated façade
opposite the Hofburg, the Imperial Palace
offended the Emperor. The architect
had to add window flower boxes.

44

45

45 Vienna, Karl-Marx-Hof, 1926
Architect: Karl Ehn
One of the first of many public housing
projects built by the City following the
establishment of the Republic after World
War I. 60% of the Viennese now live in
such housing.

344

46

47

48

49

50

51

6, 47 Vienna, Wienzeile Apartments, 898
rchitect: Otto Wagner
he façade is decorated with gilded plaster.
he interior iron elevator and stair railings
reak with tradition.

8 Vienna, Hof Pavilion, 1898
rchitect: Otto Wagner
he private underground train station built
ear the Schönbrunn Palace for the
mperor, with Art Nouveau inspired
ecoration.

**9 Vienna, Karlsplatz Underground
tation, 1898**
rchitect: Otto Wagner
he gilded iron framed structure holds walls
f white marble panels, said to be the first
on-weight bearing "curtain wall".

50 Vienna, Flood Control Building, 1906
Architect: Otto Wagner

**51, 52 Vienna, Sezession Exposition
Pavilion, 1898**
Architect: Joseph Maria Olbrich
With the famous inscription "To each era its
art and to art its freedom".

53

54

55

56

57

53-56 Vienna, Postsparkasse, 1906
Architect: Otto Wagner
Specially designed air heating columns,
light fixtures and furniture. The thick granite
exterior facing is secured with exposed
metal bolts.

57 Vienna, Candle Shop, 1964-66
Architect: Hans Hollein
The façade is entirely of jointlessly fused
aluminium sheets.

58 Vienna, Holocaust Memorial, 2000
Artist: Rachel Whiteread
The solid stone exterior is all carved
without openings. The doors are solid,
and the walls are in the shape of inverted
books - all is hidden, inaccessible and
inexplicable forever.

Switzerland

It is hard for this small country to compete with the historic architecture of its large neighbours, France, Germany and Italy. Without their war damage, however, the medieval charm of Swiss towns and the breathtaking mountainous scenery are hard to beat. There are some exceptions such as the extraordinary Einsiedeln Benedictine Abbey with its Baroque interior planned around a pilgrimage area in its centre. Modern architecture developed a strong foothold in the 1930's with the application of high quality technology and characteristically solid construction evident, particularly in their new schools and public buildings. The wealth of the country resulted in patrons commissioning some of the best progressive architects to design their houses and buildings, such as Le Corbusier and Marcel Breuer.

Outstanding amongst the local creative talents is the pioneering structural engineer Robert Maillart whose bridges span the deep chasms in the Swiss Alps and the artist and architect Max Bill.

Zurich

3

2 Bern
The Swiss capital city has a charming sequence of medieval narrow streets, similar to the old town area of Zürich (1 and 3).

3 Zurich

354

4

5

4-7 Einsiedeln, Benedictine Abbey, 1704-47

Architect: Kaspar Moosbrugger
Dominating the large town square, the church's unusual plan places the pilgrimage area in the centre of a large oval entrance space. This results in a dramatically radiating arched support structure. To increase the apparent depth of the nave is an iron screen, with lines imitating perspective effects.

8 Geneva, Vessy Bridge, 1936
Engineer: Robert Maillart
A seminal example by a pioneer of a concrete structure that is expressive of rational static forces and simultaneously achieves fine visual results.

9 Zürich, Doldertal Apartments, 1935
Architect: Marcel Breuer
The two identical residential buildings face a steep wooded river valley. They are celebrated icons of early modern architecture.

8

9

10

11

10, 11 Moscia, Koerfer House, 1963
Architect: Marcel Breuer
Built on a rugged hillside commanding a sweeping view of Lago Maggiore, the concrete structure is exposed both inside and out. It stands on granite rubble walls, which fit the house into the terrain.

12 Zürich, La Maison de l'Homme, 1967
Architect: Le Corbusier
The exhibition pavilion is the result of the private initiative of Heidi Weber and was built in a public park close to Zürich Lake. One of the few steel structures by Le Corbusier, its form is defined by two opposing umbrella-like roof forms. The brightly coloured exterior panels contrast with the off-form concrete access ramp.

Czech Republic

This small country has a varied history. Before World War I, it was a part of the Hapsburg Empire, then a joined part with its neighbour Slovakia and now on its own. It is known not only for its beautiful small towns dating from the middle ages, but also for its technologically advanced industries and universities.

The World War II German army's advance to the east caused little damage to the World Heritage old towns such as Telc, Cesky Budevice, Cesky Krumlov, etc.

Since the end of the Iron Curtain, Prague has become the treasure house of architectural heritage from Gothic, Baroque and the modern era.

St. Vitus Cathedral from the 14th Century, the Hradcany Castle's rib-vaulted King's Hall and the charming alchemists' tiny houses next to the palace, are all unique. Aside from the classical Baroque churches built in the 18th Century, the little known architect Jan Santini produced some amazing buildings such as the church in Zdar. One of the first large modern public buildings, the Pensions Institute of 1924 (architects Havlicek and Honzik) is evidence of the country being the first to adopt modern architecture wholeheartedly.

Recognised throughout the civilised world as the very icon of modern architecture is the Tugendhat House, 1929, by Mies van der Rohe, built in Brno. It is not only an aesthetic triumph, but the methods and materials used would strain the resources of today, 75 years later.

Prague
Old Town Square with the 15th Century
Tyn Church.

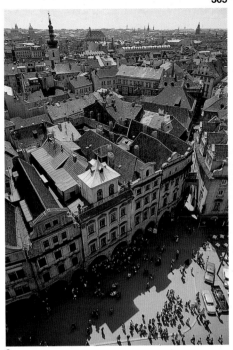
3

2 Prague, Charles Bridge, 1357-1402
Architect: Peter Parler
Connects the Old Town to the "Lesser" side
of Town. The bridge is lined with sculptures
on both sides, some of Saints, which were
a later addition.

3 Prague
View down onto the Square from the Old
Town Hall tower.

4

4 Prague, Cernin Palace

5 Prague, Castle entrance

6 Prague
Three façades in Old Town Square, dating
from 14th to 18th Century.

7

8

7, 9 Prague, St Nicholas Church, 1700
Architect: Christoph Dientzenhofer
A superbly flamboyant example of Baroque architecture inside and out.

8, 10 Prague, St Vitus Cathedral, 14th Century
Architects: Peter Parler and Matthias of Arras
The structure spanning the high nave and crossing consists of exceptionally narrow columns and high clerestory, rising to interlocking ribbed vaults.

11-12 Prague Castle, Vladislav Hall
15th-16th Century
Architect: Benedikt Rejt
The exposed curved vaulting ribs are largely
decorative and of doubtful structural value.

13, 14 Prague, Strahov Abbey and
Philosophical Hall, 18th Century
Ceiling fresco by A. F. Maulbertsch

11

12

3

4

15 Cesky Krumlov, St Vitus Church, 1439

16 Brno Cathedral, 15th Century
Architect: Anthony Pilgram

17 Kutna Hora, St Barbara Cathedral, 15th Century
Architect: Matyas Rejsek
The delicately interwoven vault ribbing.

18 Cesky Krumlov
Panoramic view from the castle over the Old Town centre.

19

21

19, 21 Cesky Krumlov
Arcaded facades on the main square.

20, 22 Telc
The main square in this World Heritage listed town is ringed by continuous arcaded buildings. Although they have different facades, the result is a harmonious totality.

23

24

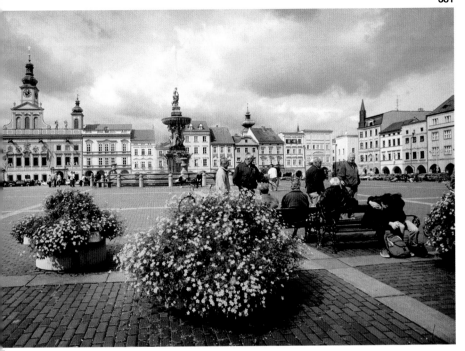

5

23 Telc

24 Slavonice
16th Century "diamond" vaulting in a
building entry court.

25 Cesky Budevice
The huge square surrounded by arcaded
buildings and the Town Hall form the
popular focus of this small town.

26, 27 Zdar, St Nepomuk Church, 1722
Architect: Jan Santini
This five-sided domed church (a UNESCO
Cultural Heritage) is based on extraordinary
geometry, which changes from the inside to
the richly sculptural exterior. Surrounding
the churchyard is a typical Santini work with
chapels of alternating concave and convex
plan outlines.

28, 30-32 Brno, Tugendhat House, 1929
Architect: Ludwig Mies van der Rohe
This house built for the Tugendhat family in 1929 is one of Mies van der Rohe's masterpieces. The free-flowing spaces are made possible by the use of technologically advanced construction for its time, such as exposed chromed steel supports and enormous areas of glass, which can be electrically lowered down below the floor. Neglected and vandalised during World War II, it is now a faithfully restored house museum, furnished with the famous tables and chairs Mies designed specially for the house. Onyx and Palisander screen walls create a sumptuously elegant atmosphere, which is an icon in modern architecture.

29 Ludwig Mies van der Rohe, 1886-1969

33 Marienbad Colonnade, 1889
Architects: Miksch and Niedzielski
This popular spa, set in a park, is typical of the late 19th Century. The long ambulatory is of ornate cast iron construction.

28

29

30

33

Hungary

This small country has a unique background, starting with the Magyar people's migration from central Asia, the language they brought (with its only parallel in Finland), the 150 year long occupation by th Turks, all contributed to a vibrant architectural development over the centuries.
After the Turks were driven out in 1686 th country came under Habsburg rule, result ing in absorption into the Austro-Hungaria Monarchy.
Budapest, the second capital in the Empi has many parallel characteristics to those of Vienna; an almost identical Opera Hous and similar palaces of members of the aristocracy.
The outstanding and most ambitious of these who built estates are members of th Esterhazy dynasty. The rivalry between th two countries is given expression in Princ Miklos Esterhazy's famous comment, vyin to outdo each other "Anything the Habsburgs can afford, I can too". After buildinc design during the 19th Century, following the modes of Classicism and Gothic Revival, a number of Hungarian architects were some of the first who practiced modern architecture in Europe. The best-known of these are two who became key figures at the German Bauhaus, Marcel Breuer in architecture and furniture desigr and Lazlo Maholy-Nagy in art.

1 Fertőd, Esterhazy Palace, 1760
Reminiscent of Vienna's Schönbrunn Palace down to the yellow-ochre exterior colouring.

2 Budapest, Heroes Square, 1886
Architect: Schickendanz
With statues of Hungary's greatest leaders from the founding of the State to the 19th Century.

3 Budapest, Neo Gothic Parliament Building „Orszaghaz", 1885-1902
Architect: Imre Steindl
Built on a dramatic waterfront site facing the Danube.

5

4 Budapest, Museum of Applied Arts, 1883-1896
Architect: Ödön Lechner
Curvilinear central interior space, to emphasise the eastern origin of the country.

5 Budapest
Cast iron candelabra on the Café Hungaria building.

6 Budapest, 19th Century
Metal gate entry into the Royal Buda Palace.

7, 10 Sopron
Tower and central Baroque Town Square.

8 Hollóko
A World Heritage picturesque village
with white houses, red roofs and cobble
stone paving.

9 CAK
A World Heritage ancient group of thatched
roof houses used as wine cellars.

6

7

Balkans

This war torn country's turbulent history reflects the architecture of its culturally diverse inhabitants. The north of the country buildings are related to the Habsburg Empires, whereas the southern cities show th results of centuries of Ottoman occupation Byzantine Domes, Minarettes and Ottoman style buildings predominate.

The most impressive cities line the Dalmatian Coast and Coastal Islands, some dating back to Roman Times. The walled towns such as Split and Dubrovnik, in spite of earthquakes and external attacks, remain as some of the most cohesive urban architectural environments anywhere.

Tragically, the famous 16th Century Mostar stone arch bridge, a historical Heritage Site was blown up in the war of 1993. It is to b rebuilt.

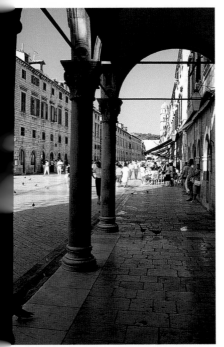

1, 2 Dubrovnik, Croatia
This dramatic coastal city seen from above
has a sheltered harbour and protective
fortified battlement walls. In spite of its
history of earthquakes, fires and the
senseless bombardments in 1991, this
World Heritage Listed city remains one of
the treasures of man's built environments.
An entrance portico and the main street.

4

3 Split, Croatia
The focus of this ancient city on the
Dalmatian Coast is the Palace of the
Emperor Diocletian (300 AD). Although
important elements remain of the Palace, it
became filled with buildings and narrow
alleys.

4 Sveti Stefan, Montenegro
This island, connected to the mainland by a
causeway is now used as a hotel.

6

7

5-7 Dubrovnik, Croatia

All streets, fountains, church towers and all
buildings are built of hard limestone and
pale yellow and light red roofing tiles. This
singular cohesive colouring creates a rare
urban consistency.

8, 9 Mostar, Bosnia-Herzegovina

The town along both sides of the river focuses on the 14th century footbridge, which
was destroyed in 1993, but hopefully will be
restored.

10

10 Pristina, Kosovo
A fine interlocking vaulted arch stone church.

11 Bled, Slovenia
A romantic island and pilgrimage church in
a lake near the Austrian border.

Bulgaria

Being on the international route from Eastern and Central Europe to Asia Minor and
the Middle East, the architecture shows
diverse influences. A strong Roman tradition left a predominance of arched structures, aqueducts, amphitheatres and ther-
mae. Byzantine domed structures recall
the long lasting invasions of Ottoman Turks
Culturally, the country has had a strong
affinity with Russia. The most distinctive
building complexes are the numerous
Monasteries throughout the country. Often
built in isolated mountainous regions, which
were liable to attack, they were built with
bland and solid high surrounding walls. Life
was turned inward onto large courtyards
lined with arched access galleries. The
focal point of the establishments is always
the Church, freestanding and sculpturally
elaborate, resulting in a distinctive island-
like totality.

1 Sofia
The city square with the Gold Domed
Alexander Nevski Cathedral, 1912, and the
central Parliament House.

2 Plovdiv
The Roman Amphitheatre built by Philip II
of Macedonia.

3,5 Plovdiv
Typical of the 19th Century revival school architecture with flamboyantly decorated curvilinear facades.

4 St Kirik Monastery
A fortified medieval monastery with an 11th Century church in the central court.

6 Rila Monastery, 13th-14th Century
This listed world monument of culture is built around a large internal court with an angular sited Byzantine church at its focus. The surrounding arcaded galleries give the only access to the monastery's rooms. For protection, the exterior walls of the complex are blank.

Russia

It was the ambition of Peter the Great to bring Russia closer to Europe that resulted in the founding of St Petersburg as the country's new capital city in 1712.

The grandiose palaces standing in huge public spaces and the spiky tower of the admiralty, built along the Neva, are the architectural highlights of the city and attest to a great urban vision. The Italian architect B.F. Rastrelli was responsible for the Hermitage Winter Palace fronting the historic palace square and gilded interiors filled with priceless artworks, the Catherine Palace and the Smolny Cathedral and Convent, all built between 1750-1760.

Rastrelli also built the Peterhof surrounded by innumerable fountains and cascades, the totality rightly called the Russian Versailles. The palace was heavily damaged in World War II but was reconstructed.

Moscow was the first city in the world to invite Le Corbusier to actually build a large government complex in the 1920's, the Centrosoyus. This was indicative of the country's promising avant-garde constructivist movement in the arts of the 1920's, exemplified by the work of Malevich, Kandinsky and Rodchenko.

In the 1930's this came to an end when Stalin stopped progress and decreed reversion to classical building forms. Several wedding-cake-like skyscrapers were built in the 1950's and remain to this day, as reminders of the absurd results of dictatorship's misguided edicts in art and architecture.

The Kremlin in Moscow contains the city's most impressive buildings. The walled precinct contains a group of 15th Century gilded domed churches, the purest of them being the vaulted Assumption Cathedral. The immense extent of Red Square with the bizarre, S. Basil's Cathedral at one end is the very centre of the city. The wealth of the 19th Century is reflected in the Gum Department Store, which forms one full length of the Square. The glass vaulted iron construction is reminiscent of earlier shopping arcades in Milan and Naples.

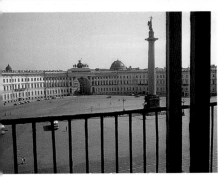

1 St. Petersburg, Hermitage Winter Palace, 1762
Architect: Bartolomeo Francesco Rastrelli
The long building facing the river on one side and the historic square on the other, is a sumptuously appointed structure with internal courtyards.

2 St. Petersburg
The historic square with the 47 m high Alexander column, commemorating the 1812 victory over Napoleon.

3 St. Petersburg
The Hermitage's river façade.

4

5

4,5 St. Petersburg, Hermitage
The monumental entrance with gilded
decor.

6 St. Petersburg
Peter the Great's "The Bronze Horseman"
statue, facing the Neva.

7 St. Petersburg
The reconstructed Peterhof Palace with
fountains playing and ballet dancers
performing celebrating an anniversary.

8 St. Petersburg
Museums and Palaces facing the Neva.

9 St. Petersburg, Catherine Palace
The long façade overlooking the park
setting.

8

9

11

12

10 St. Petersburg, Catherine Palace
Details of the reconstructed façade.

11 St. Petersburg, Catherine Palace
The Great Hall

12 St. Petersburg, Catherine Palace
The reconstructed Amber Room, which
was destroyed during World War II.

13 Smolny, Cathedral and Convent, 1764
Architect: Bartolomeo Francesco Rastrelli
The Cathedral is the centrepiece of the
large group of buildings. Rastrelli aimed
to combine Baroque detail with a forest
of onion domes of a traditional Russian
monastery.

14

16

17

14 St. Petersburg, Catherine Palace
The Grotto pavilion on the lake in the park
surrounding the Palace.

15 St. Petersburg, Catherine Palace, Pavilion in the Palace Park, 1750
Architect: Charles Cameron
The gallery building is only an arcade
to connect the palace with the park.

16,17 Moscow
Underground Stations, built in the
1930's with elaborate traditional marble
decoration to evoke an atmosphere of
palatial splendour for the masses of users.

19

18 Moscow, Kremlin, Assumption Cathedral, 1470
The beautifully proportioned arched façade is crowned with gold surfaced circular towers.

19 Moscow, Kremlin, Archangel Cathedral

20 Moscow, Red Square
The focal point of the city, with the colourfully decorated domes of St. Basil's Cathedral and people lining up to see Lenin's tomb.

21 Moscow, GUM Department Store, 1895
Architect: Alexander Pomerantsev
Along Red Square, is an elaborate complex of iron and glass vaulted shopping galleries.

Turkey

What emerges from the country's thousands of years of colonisation, wars and occupation is one amazing building, built under Emperor Justinian in about 550 AD, Hagia Sophia in Constantinople (now Istanbul).
There had been various attempts at ambitious church construction on its site for 3C years, resulting in successive structural failures. Even though the area is subject to earthquakes, Justinian's daring constructio has survived with some structural addition It remained the biggest vaulted structure until St Peter's in Rome, built some 1,000 years later.
The vast volume is based on a transition from a square structure to a circular dome supported on semicircular arches and pendentives between them. The spatial effect on the interior in its 70 metre length and the 31 metre superimposed dome is breathtaking. In 1453, the building became a mosque and in 1935, a museum.
The other landmark structure is the Blue Mosque built 1,000 years later. What Hagi Sophia has on the interior, this building ha on its exterior composition. Another architectural highlight is the restored Greek and Roman city of Ephesus, particularly the Library of Celsus. The restoration of its main façade was undertaken by the Austrian Government.
Cappadocia is an area in central Turkey which is in large parts covered with eroded mountains of Tufa, a soft volcanic stone. Over centuries people have carved spaces and caves into these and created virtual cities both inside the mountains and underground. The extreme climate of the area, intense heat and cold, make these excavated spaces, due to their constant temperature, quite hospitable in which to live and store vegetables and fruit. They create a vast sculpturesque landscape of perforated peaked mountains and valleys.

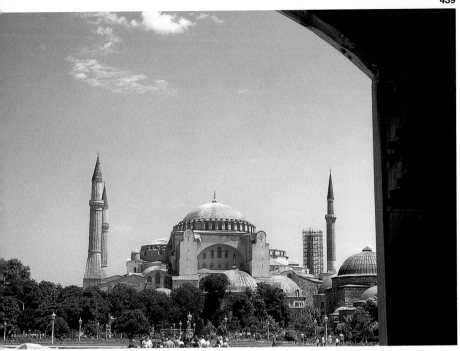

Istanbul, Hagia Sophia, 6th Century

3

4

2, 5 Istanbul, Mosque of Sultan Ahmed (Blue Mosque), 1606-16
Architect: Mehmet Aga
The forecourt is surrounded by a domed arcade leading into a square structure with heavy supporting piers. Six minarets add to a finely proportioned totality.

3 Istanbul, Hagia Sophia, 6th Century
This enormous church interior with its suspended central dome is a heroic structural feat for its time.

4 Ankara, Memorial to Atatürk, 1944-53
The country's revered leader who "brought Turkey into the 20th Century". A vast ceremonial open space is surrounded by arcades with the stripped classical style mausoleum on its axis.

6

8

6, 8 Ephesus, The Library of Celsus, 260 AD

The reconstruction and preservation of the façade were conducted by Prof. Friedmund Hueber of the Austrian Archaeological Institute. Alternating curved and triangular pediments above and flat offset entablatures below
are carried by columns, which create a scintillating façade composition.

7 Ephesus

The Roman amphitheatre built into naturally sloping ground.

9 Cappadocia

Entrances to ancient cave dwellings, cut into eroded mountains of soft Tufa, volcanic stone.

Israel

The architecture of Israel can be divided into
two parts; the ancient monuments, which
are more of religious than architectural inter
est, and the new architecture in the cities,
especially in Tel Aviv, which is a young and
rapidly developing metropolis.
The urban plan for Tel Aviv was designed
by Sir Patrick Geddes starting in 1931.
Speedy development took place following
his plan coinciding with the arrival of
German refugee immigrant architects, led
by Erich Mendelsohn.
The results are a unique example of a city
exclusively of modern architecture which
followed a clear city plan of consistent
white structures mostly built by architects
trained in the tradition of the Bauhaus. Of
particular interest are the wide boulevards
with central tree-lined pedestrian routes, an
separated traffic lanes on either side (such
as Rothschild-Avenue). The image of the cit
is one of a unified architecture of medium
height white buildings. Areas of early (50 to
80 year old) structures are now being
restored progressively to look as new. The
larger recent areas of apartments, city
office towers and university buildings are c
very high standard.

1 Jerusalem
The Jaffa Gate leading to the Old City
through the Citadel.

**2 Jerusalem, The Israel Museum Shrine
of the Books, depository of the Dead
Sea Scrolls, 1965**
*Architects: Friedrich Kiesler and Armand
Bartos*
The accessible form of the Museum Hall is
based on the profile of the ancient con-
tainer in which the scrolls were found. The
arresting sculptural exterior is clad in gloss
white ceramics.

**3 Jerusalem, The Western or
"Wailing Wall", 20 BC**
Is a remnant of the temple destroyed in 70
AD. The grand public space in front of the
wall is the most revered urban area of the
city. The gilded "Dome of Rock" 690 AD is
seen in the left background.

4

4 Jerusalem
View from the ramparts surrounding the Old
City with the Citadel's Tower of David.

5 Jerusalem
The Billy Rose sculpture garden in the Israel
Museum. Freestanding screen walls form
an open spatial environment through which
visitors can stroll. The screen walls create a
background for each individual work of art,
without visual distraction.

6 Jerusalem, The Hadassa Hospital, 1936
Architect: Erich Mendelsohn
This excellent facility was built by the emin-
ent and influential German modern architect
who had left Germany in the early 1930's.

8

9

7, 8 Tel Aviv, Rothschild-Avenue, 1920's

The town planning of the growing city of Tel Aviv was exemplary especially in the design of tree-lined wide boulevards with central pedestrian concourses and separated traffic lanes on either side.

9 Tel Aviv, Housing, 2002

The town planning and the architecture of new large housing areas is some of the most progressive anywhere. It is remarkable that such excellent new districts have come into existence during, and in spite of, the present turmoil in the country.

10 Tel Aviv

A typical boulevard lined with unified apartment buildings of the 1930's mostly built or influenced by German émigré architects. The consistency of the white modern buildings of 70 years ago is being given new life by the extensive refurbishment in progress.

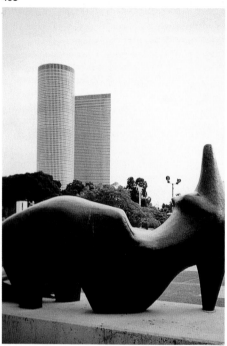

11

11, 12 Tel Aviv

Architect: Eli Attia

Three recent office skyscrapers, round, triangular and square, create an impressive
urban focus.

Jordan

With a history going back Millennia, the country which stretches from the Sea of Galilee in the North, to the Gulf of Aqaba in the South, is a veritable treasure trove of architectural highpoints.

The most spectacular of these is the rose-red ancient city of Petra. Virtually none of it buildings are freestanding, but carved into the face of the rugged sandstone mountains The approach is through a natural gorge more than 1 km long, from 2 metres wide and 200 metres deep. Emerging from this chasm, the first glimpse of the "Treasury" building takes one's breath away. The Roman influence in antiquity is evident in the finely wrought façade-architecture, some of which recalls surprising Baroque characteristics long before its time. The inhabitants were rock-cave dwellers with some spaces in the hollowed-out sand-stone, lived-in by nomadic Berbers until recent times.

The remains of the Roman town Jerash, with its curved open forum surrounded by freestanding stone columns is a superb example of Roman town planning.

Crusader strongholds such as Shobak and Ajlun in the North are exceeded in design by the desert castles of Qasar-Kharana and Qusayr Amra, serenely freestanding in the vast expanse of the eastern desert area. Their simple geometric forms and fine ston walls are recognised by UNESCO as World Heritage Sites.

To the South is the dramatic mountainous sandy Wadi-Rum area, the setting of the Lawrence of Arabia film.

1 Petra, Treasury, 1st Century AD
Approached through the Siq, a 1.2 km long narrow gorge and suddenly coming upon this rock-cut building is the ultimate thrill of discovery for the visitor.

462

2

3

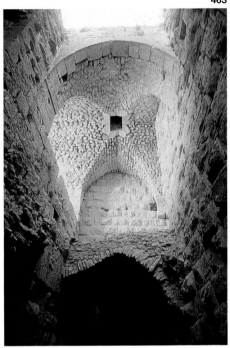

4
2-4 Ajlun, Ar-Rabad, 1185
The hilltop stone castle near the Jordan
Valley is typical of Islamic military
architecture. Its spaces are connected
by stone vaulted intersecting passages.

464

5-14 Jerash, 333 BC - 500 AD
The Roman city is entered through Hadrian's Arch, 129 AD. The oval shaped forum is defined by freestanding columns, which are connected at their capitals.

6 Temple of Artemis, 150-170 AD

7 Hadrian's Arch, 129 AD

10 Jerash
The forum's colonnade extends to define the main streets of the town, lined with monumental public buildings.

12 The Agora
Surrounding columns and stone benches create a decorative centre in this market square.

13 Nymphaeum, Temple to Artemis, 191 AD

14 Jerash
The egg and dart stone carving of a Roman entablature.

15 Irbid
A northern hillside town with ancient and recent structures, built of the same limestone, create a cohesive totality.

5

6

7

8

9

10

11

12

13

14

468

16

17

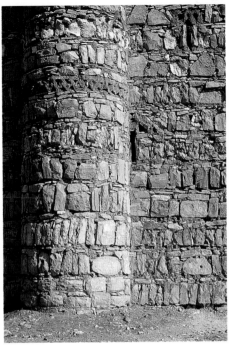

18

16 Shobak, 1115 AD
A fortified hilltop crusader castle, with
a fine silhouette.

17, 18 Qasr-Kharana
Standing alone in a treeless desert area this
impressive building has finely proportioned
exposed stone walls. The internal spaces
face an open central court.

19 Qusayr Amra, 705 AD
The barrel-vaulted structure with domes
and frescoes is influenced by Roman
precedents. It was restored and is now
a UNESCO World Heritage site.

20 Petra Treasury
Carved into the rock face on one side of a clearing this edifice creates an unforgettable image. The classical Roman façade with its broken pediment pre-empts Baroque forms of 1500 years later.

21 Petra Monastery
Standing high on a mountain top, the rock-cut structure is architecturally reminiscent to the Treasury, but faces a wide open plateau.

22 Petra
A rock-cut tomb.

23-26 Petra
Facades of rock-cut buildings surround the sides of Petra's extensive central valley.

21

22

23

24

5

6

Of all the cities of what used to be Persia, it is in Isfahan, that Islamic architecture reached its peak in the 16th Century. Located in a seemingly endless expanse of rock and sand, Isfahan lies like a huge oasis with large trees and lush foliage. Emerging from this canopy of vegetation are the inimicable shapes of domes, cupolas and minarets of the city, glistening with brightly coloured geometric patterned ceramic exteriors.

The focal point of the city is the half a kilometre long central square, the Meydan, surrounded by domed structures. At its short end stands the blue Imam Mosque. Upon entering its atrium, the building is turned at forty-five degrees, which creates a strong visual opposition to the rectangular, often water filled reflecting surface of the Meydan.

At the opposite end of the long surface of the square is the gateway to the ancient bazaar with its top lit, vaulted passages filled with shopping stalls.

1 Isfahan, Imam Mosque, 1612-30
Reflected at the end of the water filled Meydan focal square of Isfahan.

2 Isfahan
Plan of the Meydan Square

2

4

3 Isfahan
View on to the Meydan from the roof of a
galleried arcade.

4 Isfahan
Arched decorated entry portico.

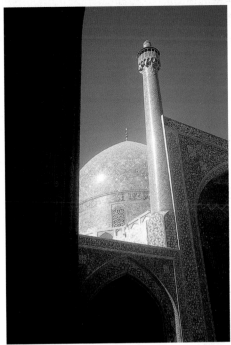

6

5 Isfahan
The ancient bazaar, a high, top-lit vaulted
structure with stalls lining the criss-crossing
passages.

6 Isfahan
The pointed dome and minaret of the Imam
Mosque.

7 Isfahan
The Masjit-i-Imam with typical geometric
repeated ceramic surfaces, which permit
infinite numbers of permutations.

Malta

The three isolated rocky islands between Sicily and North Africa have a rich history of habitation going back to 3000 BC. Home to the Phoenicians, their conquests of Carthage, Rome and Spain over the centuries, has left a rich heritage of unique stone architecture. Sought by all with ambitions to control the Mediterranean, it became the target of fierce bombardments in World War II.

In spite of that, Malta withstood attacks from sea and air and yet maintained its ancient character with some fine Renaissance churches, Government buildings an palaces remaining. Built of beautiful local white limestone, which imparts a unity to the whole built environment, the stone is soft and easily quarried. With age it dries and becomes very hard.

The solid rocky shores of Malta constitute natural fortifications, which give the islands its unique appearance. The narrow streets of traditional row houses are characterised by projecting fully enclosed, roofed and glazed balconies which have their origins in Islamic cultures. They used to be fully screened for privacy.

1 Gozo
This outlying island of Malta, with its ancient fortified capital, Victoria.

2 Valletta
Facades with characteristic projecting bay windows.

3 Marsaschlock
A waterfront fishing village with its colourfully painted boats.

4 Valletta
View from the hilltop, Siege Bell memorial to the unknown soldier of World War II with the Grand Harbour of Valletta beyond.

5 Valletta
A Valletta street with enclosed balconies, which are of old Turkish origin and were obscured with blinds for privacy.

6 Valletta, The Auberge de Castille, 1740
Architects: Girolamo Cassar, 1574, redesigned by Andrea Belli, 1741, now the Prime Minister's office.

7 Valletta
The Grand Harbour

3

4

5

6

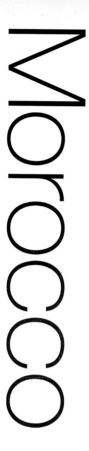

Morocco

Lying between the Mediterranean and the Sahara, the country is traversed by the dramatic Atlas Mountains, snow capped most of the year. Historically inhabited by a resilient Berber population, the country has never been subjugated by numerous invaders.

Of particular architectural interest are the ancient fortified hill-top towns and the villages in valleys of the foothills on both sides of the Atlas Mountains. Built of mud brick walls with flat roofs, they create uniform coloured unique abstract patterns in the mostly dry and barren landscape.

The fortified towns with tall defence towers are the Kasbahs built mostly in the dry river valleys of the Draa and Dades. The best known of these is at Ait Benhaddou, which is a popular movie location.

The cities of Morocco have densely populated centres (the "Medina") with alleys rather than streets barely more than a metre wide. Focal points are the Souq or bazaars, the commercial backbone of the city in which workshops, wool stores and living quarters have not changed in centuries. The uninitiated visitor is easily lost in this labyrinth, lacking any street names.

The imperial cities of Meknes, Fes and Marrakesh, have architectural focal points of the surrounding walls with protective towers and the distinctive design of palaces and mosques.

1 Taroudant
The town is surrounded by magnificent crenellated red mud walls.

2 Tioulit

A protected town in the Anti-Atlas.

3, 4 Dades Valley

Red mud brick villages of the Dades Valley create even coloured rectangular abstract patterns seen against the snow covered High Atlas Mountains.

5 Ait Benhaddou, Kasbah

An impressive assembly of tapered high towers surrounding courtyards with high walls.

3

4

6 Meknes, The Rouah
Ruins of the 17th Century royal stables, which at one time housed 12,000 horses.

7 Marrakesh
Protective city walls.

8 Meknes
Detail of the King's palace gates of gold.

9 Moulay Idriss
Morocco's most important pilgrimage destination containing the 17th Century mausoleum of Moulay Idriss I.

7

8

USA

From the early days of European migration to America, in the 17th Century, the prototype of buildings was based on English precedent, even if mostly translated into the locally available material in abundance: timber. The European cultural background continued and reached a high point under President Thomas Jefferson who was influenced by European classic architecture during his term as America's Ambassador to France. He was a naturally gifted amateur architect, evidenced in his exemplary design for the Campus of the University of Virginia in 1819-26.

American architects in the 19th Century followed the English and French prevalent stylisms until the Industrial Revolution when dramatic advances were made technically and aesthetically. The use of iron enabled buildings to rise higher, aided by the development of the Otis elevator. Economic expansion and consequent wealth allowed architects like Louis Sullivan and Frank Lloyd Wright to unfold their inventive genius of structural daring and a new spaciousness in their buildings. It helped skyscrapers reach unprecedented heights in the early 20th Century.

The arrival of European émigré architects in the 1930's who could no longer teach or build under the rise of the totalitarian Nazi regime, Walter Gropius who founded the influential Bauhaus with former teachers Marcel Breuer the pioneer of steel furniture, renowned teacher and designer Mies van der Rohe, its last director, were all invited to teach at Harvard and I.I.T. in Chicago and obtained increasingly important commissions to build. This had immeasurable influence on the young generation and large competing firms of architects such as Skidmore Owings & Merrill. The 1950's-1970's architecture of high quality reached its zenith. Under the pressure toward commercial and advertising newness, "a new architecture every Monday morning", brought fads of styles into existence, fed by the media who published and listened to influential, articulate but opportunistic practitioners.

The cultural base which brought European Modern Architecture into existence was

missing and was soon replaced with fashions
of historistic decorative modes in the '70's
and 80's, ie. postmodernism, deconstruct-
vism, etc, all meaningless labels coined by
non-practising academics and journalists.
As all fads, these soon cloyed the appetite
for "newness" and disappeared.
Nevertheless, important progressive build-
ngs, skyscrapers for successful corporation,
museums, fine houses and interiors mostly
for the wealthy, came into existence, by
Breuer, Neutra, Mies van der Rohe, Pei,
Saarinen, Meier, and the most brilliant,
Frank Lloyd Wright. Le Corbusier designed
his only U.S. building at Harvard University.
By the end of the 20th Century and the
death of pioneering architects, a hiatus of
aesthetic development gave way to aim-
essness, fake historicism and a search for
elusive convincing directions.
Driven mainly by market forces, in contrast
to most European countries, no large scale
town planning or high quality social housing
have come into existence in the USA.

1

**1 New York, Rockefeller Center,
1929-40**
*Architects: Reinhard & Hofmeister with
Raymond Hood*
Simultaneously with the Empire State and
the Chrysler Tower, this landmark of New
York was built during the Great Depression.
It consists of nine various height buildings
with the 70-storey RCA Tower its centrepiece. What is admirable in the complex
are the large open pedestrian spaces
which have remained a magnet attracting
people to its malls and plazas.

3

4

2-8 Charlottesville, University of Virginia, 1819-26

Architect: Thomas Jefferson

The symmetrical U-shaped central space terminates in the Roman Pantheon-like library building in this serenely beautiful environment. Five double-storey pavilions connected by low classical colonnades contain teaching and living accommodation. Jefferson was a naturally gifted amateur architect. His direct and ingenious planning was exemplary, not only aesthetically, but by inventive structural devices such as the long and thin self-supporting wave-shaped brick walls achieving much with little effort and material.

9, 10 Chicago, Illinois, Carson Pirie Scott, 1899-1904
Architect: Louis Sullivan

This influential pioneer architect was the first to give expressive strength to early skyscraper buildings which were based on iron skeleton construction. The ground level exterior is encased in cast iron decorative panels, the American counterpart to European art-nouveau of the time.

11 Chicago, The Rookery, 1885-88
Architects: Daniel H. Burnham, John Wellborn Root, Frank Lloyd Wright (reconstruction)

The exposed iron structure supporting the central glazed court's roof is an example of progressive engineering design in the 19th Century.

10

11

12

12,15 Oak Park, Illinois, Unity Temple, 1904-07
Architect: Frank Lloyd Wright
One of the first "binuclear" or "H plans" later used extensively by others, whereby the main hall and subsidiary spaces are separate and connected with a narrowed entrance link. The powerful solid concrete building has a clear structural expression in the hall, emphasised by the source of daylight. Deep glazed coffers in the roof and horizontal windows placed between the corner supporting elements.

14 Frank Lloyd Wright 1867-1959

13,16 Chicago, Illinois, Robie House, 1906-10
Architect: Frank Lloyd Wright
This is one of Wright's most famous works, characterised by hugely cantilevered low slung roof planes, interlocking volumes and planes and sweeping horizontals.

13

14

15

16

17

18

19

20

17 Chicago, Illinois, Crown Hall, I.I.T., 1950-56
Architect: Mies van der Rohe
The main floor of this architecture school
consists of a single large space, supported
by an external steel frame and enveloped
in glass. It is one of Mies' most expressive
concepts of a powerful minimal structure.

18 Chicago, Illinois, John Hancock Tower, 1965-70, 1968-75
Architects: Skidmore, Owings & Merrill
The huge tapering tower contains both
commercial office space and apartments.
The external structural cross bracing gives
a distinctive character to the building.

19 Chicago, Federal Center, 1970
Architect: Mies van der Rohe
This typical black framed curtain wall tower
is made unique by the placing of the large
orange coloured Alexander Calder stabile
sculpture.

20 Chicago, Sears Tower, 1974
Architects: Skidmore, Owings & Merrill
Until 1996 it was the tallest building in
the world. Its silhouette is made up of a
cluster of smaller towers of different heights,
generated by the different heights of the
groups of elevators.

512

21

21 Washington DC, Dulles International Airport, 1958-62
Architect: Eero Saarinen
The sweeping catenary roof structure is supported by outward leaning concrete pylons and steel tension cables hung between them, resulting in a huge column-free space.

22 Washington DC, Monument
The focal axis of the capital with its obelisk as seen from the Lincoln Memorial, 1911-1922, Architect Henry Bacon, is based on the Washington Plan by Pierre Charles L'Enfant in 1791.

22

'3

23,24 Washington DC, East Wing, National Gallery of Art, 1975

Architect: Ieoh Ming Pei

The basis of this superbly designed monumental building is triangular geometry and forms derived from it. The central main space is covered with a glass roof from which a red Alexander Calder mobile sculpture hangs and is kept in constant motion by the ventilation system.

25 Ieoh Ming Pei, *1917

26 New Harmony, Indiana, The Atheneum, 1975-79

Architect: Richard Meier

Built in a historic town founded by a Utopian community in 1815, this is a centre for visitors' orientation and community cultural events. The elaborate spatial complex contains exhibition areas and an auditorium all connected by internal access ramps. The generous glass areas allow views over the lushly planted surroundings and the nearby Wabash River.

24

25

27

28

9

27, 28 Collegeville, Minn., St John's Abbey and University, 1953-70
Architect: Marcel Breuer
The folded concrete Abbey Church is supported by ground level columns with glass walls between that admit daylight to the monumental interior which is tapered both vertically and horizontally. The dramatic freestanding bell banner straddles the entrance.

29, 30 Muskegon, Mich., St. Francis de Sales Church, 1961-67
Architect: Marcel Breuer
Rising from a rectangular plan at the ground, three trapezoidal planes form the front and rear walls and the roof. Two twisting hyperbolic paraboloid side walls complete the enclosure. The unique interior contains a freestanding balcony.

31 Marcel Breuer 1902-1981

31

0

32

32, 33 Syracuse, NY, Everson Museum, 1968

Architect: Ieoh Ming Pei

The contrast between the minimalist rectilinear sculptural exterior and the interior could not be greater. The flying cantilevers outside give way to constantly changing spatial excitements inside. The main space is traversed by a curvilinear stair and ramp with linear sources of daylight.

33

34

35

34,35 Fort Worth, Texas, Kimbell Museum of Art, 1972
Architect: Louis Kahn
Composed of six parallel concrete vaults which span the whole length of the structure, the "servant" spaces between them allowed variations of displays between the top lit galleries within the long vaults.

36 Bear Run, Pennsylvania, Fallingwater, Kaufmann House 1936
Architect: Frank Lloyd Wright
This is Wright's world-famous house, cantilevered over a gushing waterfall in the most beautiful wild natural setting. The vertical rough stone piers support daringly hovering horizontal concrete elements of terraces and suspended spaces. Even though romantic in character, the off-white house is clearly influenced by European modern architecture of the time.

37 San Francisco Houses
These vernacular 19th Century houses with carved timber decorations give whole districts of the city their unmistakable character.

38 San Francisco, Cal., Office Building, 1890
An early steel framed city building with a glass curtain wall façade, long before this was re-introduced by European émigré architects, 50 years later.

38

39 San Francisco, Cal., Russell Residence, 1948
Architect: Erich Mendelsohn
One of the few American buildings by Mendelsohn, this lavish residence is built overlooking an expansive public park.

39

40 Oakland, Cal., Oakland Museum, 1961
Architect: Kevin Roche
The museum consists of low pavilions, connected by landscaped roofs which create the impression of a large stepped park.

41 San Francisco, Cal., Crown Zellerbach Building, 1957
Architect: Skidmore, Owings & Merrill
This office tower is freestanding in landscaped grounds. A circular low bank building with a folded plate roof creates a focus for occupants looking down.

40

41

42

43

44

42 Los Angeles, Cal., Lovell House, 1928
Architect: Richard Neutra
This well-known house is one of the first examples of uncompromising modern architecture in America. Its light steel frame construction and multi-level spacious interiors influenced much later design in the U.S. and Europe.

43 Palm Springs, Cal., Kaufmann House, 1946
Architect: Richard Neutra
Based on a pin-wheel plan, the different wings allow individual panoramic views of the surrounding mountains and desert scenery to every room.

44 Los Angeles, Cal., Charles Ennis House, 1924
Architect: Frank Lloyd Wright
This hillside house, built of decorated cast concrete blocks, recalls Mayan stone carved architecture.

45-47 Los Angeles, Cal., The Paul Getty Center and Museum, 1984-97
Architect: Richard Meier
Located on a hilltop above the city, this complex of buildings is the most elaborate anywhere dedicated to art. The various pavilions contain study centres and museums, grouped around large open spaces with gardens, fountains and restaurants. Most buildings are clad in white metal, but some are of split travertine stone resulting in deeply textured surfaces under strong sunlight.

45

46

47

48

48 Boston, Mass., Quincy Market, 1976
Architect: Ben Thompson
This successful urban renewal project
revitalises an early 19th Century market and
warehouse area (designed by Alexander
Parris).

49,51,52 Lincoln, Mass., Walter Gropius House, 1937
Architects: Walter Gropius & Marcel Breuer
This revolutionary house is the first work
by these two recently appointed influential
Harvard Professors. The simple rectilinear
outline of the building is sculpted with
hollowed out, recessed spaces, stone
walls and screens. The angled entrance
is recalled in an opposing slanting wall in
the living area.
Other than in books, it is the first deeply
impressive masterpiece of modern
architecture that Gropius' students have
seen (including myself).
Photo 51, the 1946 photo is the earliest
taken, in this book.

49

50

51

52

50 Cohasset, Mass., Hagerty House, 1938

Architects: Walter Gropius, Marcel Breuer
The entrance side of the seaside villa faces the ocean on the other side with large areas of glass. The two sides are joined by the open ground space under the suspended part of the house. The resulting landscaped open area is enclosed with stone walls.

53

54

53,54 New Canaan, Conn., Glass House, 1949

Architect: Philip Johnson

On a visit in 1955, Marcel Breuer (see photo) took me to see this steel framed glass pavilion. It was the first of such totally glazed houses in the USA. It is built in an extensive park-like setting and was later joined by other small buildings, a sculpture pavilion, an underground museum and a guest house.

Mies van der Rohe had sketched such a glass house in 1934 and built the elegant Farnsworth House in Plano, Ill. in 1951.

55,56 Boston, Mass., Museum of Fine Arts, 1981

Architect: Ieoh Ming Pei

This stone clad addition to the large existing museum complex has a central glass vaulted spine from which exhibition spaces emanate horizontally and vertically.

57,58 Cambridge, Mass., Carpenter Center for the Visual Arts, 1963

Architect: Le Corbusier

Built at Harvard University, this is Le Corbusier's only building in North America. Studio spaces are located on either side of a flowing access ramp which penetrates the building and connects two parallel streets. Activities in the studios are visible to all who pass through the building.

The south facing spaces are equipped with external sun louvres which add texture to the off-form concrete building. The Center is one of Le Corbusier's most stunning, sculpturally and constructionally. It is also the best maintained of all his buildings.

55

56

57

58

59 Manhattan, New York, Wall Street
The financial business district's very narrow
streets are lined with skyscrapers dating
from the early 20th Century. The high rise
buildings dwarf the church tower which
was once a tall landmark.

**60 New York, George Washington
Bridge**
This advanced engineering feat of a steel
suspension bridge across the Hudson River
was built in the 1930's. When Mies van der
Rohe was interviewed in 1957 and asked
what he considered the best building in
New York, he named this bridge.
This photo was taken in 1946 by stopping
the car on the bridge and climbing onto the
footpath!

60

61

62

61,62 New York, Museum of Modern Art, 1939

Architects: Philip Goodwin & Edward Durrell Stone

This culturally important museum started as a plain translucent stone fronted structure. It has undergone many alterations and additions over the years, the best of which is the fine sculpture garden by Philip Johnson.

A total rebuilding and enlargement is in progress.

63, 64, 65 New York, Solomon R. Guggenheim Museum, 1959

Architect: Frank Lloyd Wright

Wright's most celebrated building is based on an extraordinary concept, some 15 years in development. The central top lit atrium is surrounded by spiral gallery spaces, which were much criticised due to the sloping floors and limited ceiling height. With the completion of Wright's original rectilinear wing, with high spaces (Architect: C. Gwathmey) the museum functions well and is more popular than ever.

63

64

66

66, 68 New York, Whitney Museum of American Art, 1966

Architect: Marcel Breuer
Placed on a small corner site, the grey granite clad square building steps out toward the top to leave space for an outdoor sculpture court below street level. Unique trapezoidal windows admit daylight to the gallery floors. The beautiful Alexander Calder exhibition in 1976 shows the success of the flexible display lighting from the squared concrete grid ceiling.

67, 69 New York, Seagram Building, 1958

Architect: Ludwig Mies van der Rohe
Mies' masterpiece is recognised as the quintessential skyscraper of the 20th Century. The tower is set back from Park Avenue, creating a public space, on which huge sculptures are often displayed. The minimalist "almost nothing" design of the tower asserts its monumentality and longevity by being clad in bronze.
Even wall-wash lighting, developed for the building by Richard Kelly was used for the first time on the high travertine clad entrance walls.

68

69

538

70

71

72

73

70 New York, United Nations Development, 1969
Architect: Kevin Roche
An early example of tower architecture abandoning a routine rectilinear silhouette.

71, 74 New York, Chase Manhattan Bank, 1957-60
Architects: Skidmore, Owings & Merrill (Gordon Bunshaft)
The architecture of this quality headquarters office building offers a neutral background, but gains stature by the placement of major sculptures at ground level by Dubuffet, and in a sunken court by Noguchi.
The Head of the Bank, David Rockefeller's office continues this theme; elegant minimalism, enriched with large colourful artworks.

72, 73 New York, The Ford Foundation, 1968
Architects: Eero Saarinen & Kevin Roche
This headquarters building maximises the opportunity offered by its site adjacent to a park. The central high atrium is overlooked from the L-shaped office floors and faces the other two full height glass walls toward the park. High Eucalyptus Trees in the atrium extends the park inside.

74

75 World Trade Center Towers, 1966-73
Architect: Minoru Yamasaki

For some 30 years the 100-storey twin office towers were the most visible landmarks of Manhattan. On September 11, 2001, they were destroyed in a terrorist attack by jet aircraft being driven into their sides, causing an inferno, which killed some 3,000 people.

The world asked - how could this have happened?

When visiting the buildings during construction in 1970, I remember being amazed at the exclusive use of lightweight building materials. Its steel structure consisted of closely spaced exterior columns and 20 m floor beams spanning to the elevator core. No concrete was used around firestairs or elevator shafts, in favour of layers of plasterboard.

The immense heat generated by the impact explosion of jet fuel, weakened the steel structure to such an extent that it caused the progressive collapse of both towers in a short time.

Nevertheless, the structural steel design of the buildings is ingenious and given normal usage would have lasted indefinitely, excluding such an outrageous terrorist attack.

However, my contention is that concrete buildings would have been damaged by the impact, but would not have collapsed.

Canada

There are many fine 19th century public buildings and modern city towers in Canada, mostly adhering to American prototypes in the large cities of Toronto and Montreal. There is however a distinct French influence historically in Eastern Canada, particularly Quebec City. The only time I spent there was during World War II, without opportunities to take photographs, as I was behind barbed wire as an 'enemy alien' internee. In recent years I did visit an outstanding building at the University of British Columbia in Vancouver.

1, 2 Vancouver, Museum of Anthropology, 1976
Architect: Arthur Erickson
Based on local timber tradition, the concrete structure consists of post and beam vertical frame members connected with glass wall and roof infills. The dramatic naturally lit interiors allow for an unusually fine display of the museums collections.

1

Mexico

Mexico has been the home of numerous civilisations for over 3000 years. The Pre-Hispanic cultures had reached a high level when they were destroyed by the Spanish conquistadores in only a few years. Christianity imposed on the population left some fine 16th and 17th Century European architecture, especially the stone churches, palaces and public buildings in the cities. Spanish in origin, their modifications even extend the European originals with highly decorated gilded interiors and alters.

What I found to be the most remarkable and memorable is the ancient Mayan architecture around Oaxaca and on the Yucatan peninsula in such centres as Uxmal and Chichen Itza. The planning and compositions of the structures that remain seem to generate a particular affinity to our own time's visual concerns.

The buildings and monuments have beautifully proportioned openings and simple façades of minimal outline which are covered, in controlled areas only, with geometric stone carvings. The steeply sloping pyramids and their relationship to the long rectangular structures continue these compositions in their site placement. Mexico's modern architecture is different to contemporary American or European work, which is particularly evident in the work of Luis Barragán and Ricardo Legorreta. Their large scale and unadorned dramatically coloured wall surfaces seem to recall the country's ancient buildings.

545

1 Uxmal, The Ruler's Palace, 600-900 AD
The stone carved building is in the Mayan Puuc style.

2 Mitla
4th Century Zapotec recessed stone carved opposing patterns.

3 Chichén Itzá, Pyrámide de Kukulkan, 800 AD
A fine geometric silhouette stone building is of Mayan religious significance with sacred vault spaces within.

1

2

3

4

4-7 Chichén Itzá, 1000 AD
Surrounding stone buildings are seen from
the top of the Pyramid; the long parallel
walls of a ball court with projecting stone
"goal" rings and the "Temple of the
Warriors" with a remaining group of a
Thousand stone columns.

8

9

10

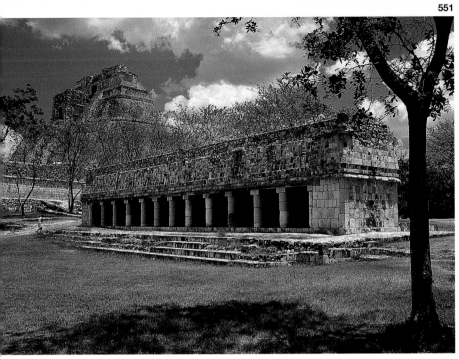

551

-11 Uxmal, C600-900 AD
ne well preserved stone buildings are of
most impressive architectural design. The
te planning and disposition of the
ructures create admirable spaces and
stas between them.

12

12-15 Uxmal, C600-900 AD

Grouped around a central pyramid are long
structures arranged to form large open
courtyards between them. The placement
of openings in the facades and particularly
the design and proportions of the sculpted
stone surfaces are some of the most
memorable in Mexico.

13

14

15

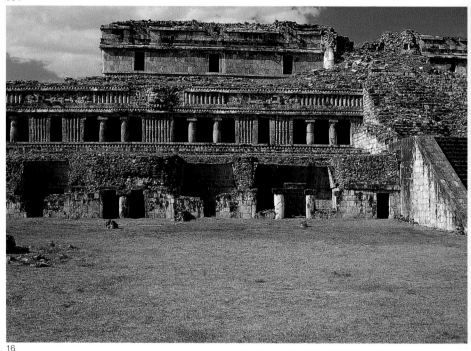

16

16-18 Sayil, El Palacio

The only three-tiered Mayan building has an 85 metre long façade decorated with grouped columns and sculpted friezes of masks. The Mayans did not know arch construction, evidenced by the collapse of the outer portion of the steeply stepped stone ground level galleries.

17

18

19

19 Dzibilchaltun
The 130 metre long palace entry steps are in fine condition, for their over 1000 year life. The Danish architect, Jørn Utzon, cites them as his inspiration for the wide entrance stairs to the Sydney Opera House.

20 Teotihuacan, 150 - 600 AD
The site for this ancient Aztec city is 50 km north of Mexico City. It was once the capital of Mexico's largest Pre-Hispanic empire. The focal structures in this vast linear development are two pyramids, the largest 70 metres high, is dedicated to the sun, the smaller to the moon. The surrounding stepped structures were once colourfully painted.

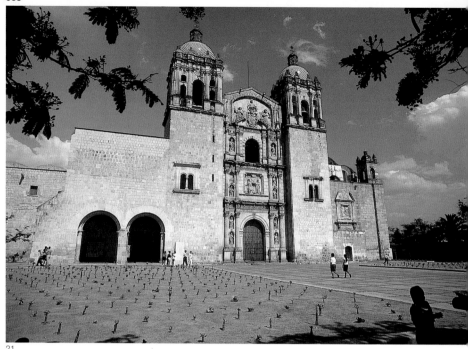

21

21 Oaxaca, Church of Santo Domingo, 1570

This splendid 16th Century church was built by the Conquistadores. The large flat stone wall surfaces concentrate the onlooker's view onto the finely carved central entrance tract.

22 Mexico City, Zócalo

With each side more than 200 metres long, this open space is one of the world's largest city squares. On its north side stands the huge Metropolitan Cathedral, which has long been beset with problems of uneven settlement into the soft ground below. The 16th Century typically Spanish Renaissance Building is covered with elaborate carved figures around its entrances, although the interior is disfigured with seemingly permanent scaffolding.

23

23 Mexico City, Palacio Nacional, 16th Century

The long beautiful façade of this focal building of the Mexican Government takes up one side of the Zocalo. It contains dramatic murals by Diego Rivera (photo taken in 1948).

24 Mexico City, Metropolitan Cathedral, 16th Century

The highly decorated and gilded recessed interior space of the altar is reminiscent of Spanish church architecture of the time.

24

25

26

27

25-27 Mexico City, Anthropological Museum, 1964
Architect: Pedro Ramírez Vazquez
The large complex of exhibition wings creates an open plaza with a huge umbrella-like fountain supported by only one column. The excellent exhibits depict Mexico's history with models of ancient Aztec cities and carved facades.

28

29

28,30 Mexico City, San Cristobal Stable and House, 1968
Architect: Luis Barragán
This large complex of brilliantly coloured freestanding pavilions, house, stables and screen walls, create a rich spatial-sculptured totality. A pond and gushing fountain are in the exercise yard for the owners' thoroughbred horses.

29 Mexico City, Luis Barragán's Own House, 1947
This unassuming modest house of the architect is full of surprises in the complex interior spaces and their natural light sources. The library's minimal composition has an open timber stair reaching the upper floor between two opposing white walls.

31 Mexico City, Casa Gilardi Indoor Swimming Pool, 1978
Architect: Luis Barragán
The pool is composed of blue, red and white smooth and textured wall and column surfaces. The colours change with the ripple of the water and create an unexpected translucence. To the user it must be a swimming experience through a work of art.

32 Luis Barragán 1902-1988

30

31

32

33

34

33 Mexico City, San Angel Casa Prieto Lopez, 1950
Architect: Luis Barragán
This house has a typical Mexican entry courtyard surrounded by brightly coloured walls. The inside spaces interact beautifully with large single pane windows opening onto tranquil gardens.

34 Mexico City, Olympic Sports Palast, 1958
Engineer: Felix Candela
The ingenious space frame structure expresses its triangulated protruding elements, which results in a uniquely sculptural exterior.

35 Mexico City, Centro National de las Artes, 1994
Architect: Ricardo Legorreta
The access stair, leading to the buildings of the centre, is typical of Mexican modern architecture which uses brilliant coloured walls.

36 Mexico City, Satellite City Towers, 1957
Architect: Luis Barragán and Artist: Mathias Goeritz
These five towers were designed as a landmark for a new satellite city. They stand on an open plaza in the centre of an expressway. Their varying heights, 30 to 50 metres, and different triangular shapes and bright colours create a powerful image seen from afar and differently from any direction. I consider this work to be the finest urban sculpture, anywhere.

Equador

1,2 Quito

On my way from the USA to Australia via South America in 1948, I stopped briefly in the capital, Quito.

Located on the Equator at 2800 metres height in the Andes, the city, founded in the 16th Century, was built on the ruins of one of the capitals of the Inca Empire.

The main square, built by the Spanish conquerors, is surrounded by fine European Renaissance and Baroque structures which combine elements of indigenous and mestizo influences. A characteristic of the architecture is the contrasting combination of large areas of white-washed walls with roughly hewn and carved natural stone. Today it would be impossible to photograph this serene colonial setting; the city has been extended with tall structures on the skyline. Nevertheless, Quito has been declared a UNESCO World Heritage Site.

1

2

Peru

The truly outstanding and memorable site in Peru is the "Lost City of the Incas", Machu Picchu, which the marauding Spanish Conquistadores never discovered. Located some 2400 metres high up in the Andes it straddles a mountainside in a spectacular setting.

It was inhabited from the 14th to 16th Centuries by a particularly constructive Pre-Hispanic Andean society that left evidence of their aesthetic creativity. Machu Picchu was home to some 1,000 to 2,000 people, who created an amazing environment of a city meticulously planned and built to incorporate housing and agricultural terraces. Public open spaces and long flights of stairs connect different districts.

Culminating in the high up "Temple of the Sun" the entirety is like an enormous sculpture consisting of man-made and natural elements in a particularly sympathetic relationship.

The capital city of the area, Cuzco, gives evidence of its Inca origins by its stone ruins and the Spanish colonial architecture. On the outskirts of town are the remains of a fort, built of cut-stone blocks fitted together so perfectly that no mortar was required. The interlocking irregular shapes of the enormous blocks preserved the walls for centuries, even though the area is known for frequent earthquakes.

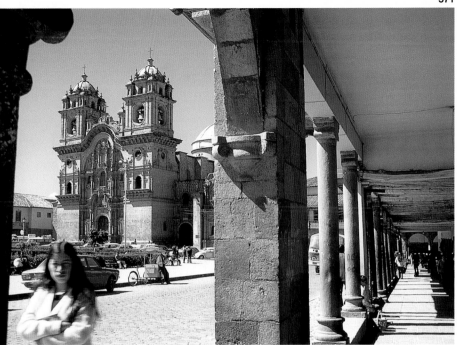

1 Cuzco, Cathedral
The focal point of the city's central square
s a fine piece of 16th Century Spanish
Baroque architecture with elaborate pure
gold interior decorations.

3

4

2-4 Machu Picchu

The Inca city high up in the Andes Mountains
with houses and agricultural terraces
ingeniously connected by long flights of
stone steps.

5 Cuzco

Inca fortification walls of tightly fitted blocks
of stone which have resisted earthquakes
due to their interlocking shapes.

Argentina

Symbolised by its capital, Buenos Aires, which is rightly referred to as the "Paris of South America", a city that has a strong European feeling in its architecture and planning. In the early years of the 20th Century it was a wealthy country evidenced by the extravagant public buildings, squares, its opera house and the extraordinary high-rise apartment towers that line the big avenues and express the strong Latin flair in their architecture, combining classical stylism with uniquely exuberant cornices and domed tops.
The huge scale of the city is particularly evidenced by Avenue 9 de Julio, said to be the widest street in the world, with its centrally placed obelisk and 8 traffic lanes on each side.
In total contrast to the monumental structures of the city, the La Boca area on the waterfront has small tin clad houses painted in all colours of the rainbow. In the nearby town of La Plata, Le Corbusier designed a house and office for a doctor, overlooking a park. Supported by a grid of circular pilotis, the surgery facing the street and the house at the rear are connected by ramps cutting through between the two separate structures, which generate fascinating outdoor/indoor spatial effects

1 Buenos Aires, Plaza de Mayo
The large civic square of the city used for public celebrations and demonstrations is lined with important buildings including the impressive Casa Rosada, the President's Palace.

4

5

2 Buenos Aires, Avenue 9 de Julio
This huge central avenue was built in 1936 to commemorate the 400th anniversary of Buenos Aires as the capital city. It is the widest street in the world with 8 traffic lanes on each side.

3 Buenos Aires
The typical elaborately decorated high-rise apartment towers from the time when Argentina was one of the wealthiest countries in the world.

4, 5 Buenos Aires, La Boca
The colourful district of tin-clad buildings near the waterfront.

6 Le Plata, Dr Currutchet House, 1949
Le Corbusier's only building in Argentina. The separated surgery and house wings are intertwined with intriguing spatial effects.

Brazil

The Portuguese architectural influence was paramount during the colonial days of the country from the 16th to the 19th Centuries. The historically protected cities such as Ouro Preto are rich in fine 17th Century Baroque churches. Although these are mostly well protected and worth visiting, the architectural focus of Brazil is in its modern architecture. This is what I was determined to experience during my stay there on route to Australia in 1948. During three months working with Oscar Niemeyer, the dramatic developments of his architecture had a lasting affect on me. At that time, soon after World War II, there was virtually no comparable modern architecture in the USA and buildings such as the new Ministry of Education in Rio were overwhelmingly convincing as the appropriate architecture for our time.

Gropius, in his writings, referred to Niemeyer rather disparagingly as the Paradiesvogel (Bird of Paradise) of architecture. The huge number of completed buildings has a certain flamboyance and curvilinearity in common, which recall the qualities of Brazil's colonial Baroque period. Undoubtedly influenced by Le Corbusier (who visited Brazil in the 1930's) in the essentials of planning and structure, Niemeyer's work has a disarming directness and clarity of concept that is raised to the level of a unique art form. His appointment to design a new capital city of Brazil led to an unsurpassed large scale planning solution (in collaboration with Lucio Costa) and groupings of buildings without equal. As an example, there is no need for, nor were any traffic lights planned in this city where the ingenious road system makes these redundant.

One of his latest works (at age over 90!) is the Museum in Niteroi. This daring concept and structure is beyond belief or description. After a visit one feels confident that there is hope for our time, that architecture will develop into an art form that can take its place alongside the finest man has ever built in the past.

1

1 Rio de Janeiro, Copacabana

This is part of one of the most beautiful
cities in the world. Copacabana is the
best known of several beachfronts with its
great sweep of a sandy beach edged by
a parallel row of tall buildings. Steep, bare
granite mountains such as the "Sugarloaf",
form the dramatic background.

2 Drawing by Oscar Niemeyer,

characteristic of his flamboyant curvilinear
architecture.

2

3-5 Rio de Janeiro, Ministry of Education, 1941
Architects: Le Corbusier, Oscar Niemeyer and others
This pioneering structure demonstrates the effective use of adjustable horizontal louvre sun protection on its fully glazed northern façade. The 10 m high open ground level portico is adorned with a tile (Azulejos) mural by Portinari.

6 Oscar Niemeyer, *1907

4

5

6

7

8

7-10 Pampulha, Mina Gerais, Recreational Buildings and a Church built around a Lake, 1943

Architect: Oscar Niemeyer
Near Bello Horizonte, the capital of the State of Minas Gerais, a restaurant, yacht club, a church (with a tile mural by Portinari) and a casino, were built on the shore of an artificial lake. They represent a display of mature modern Brazilian architecture by Niemeyer.

11 Brasilia, The Capital, 1957-60

Architect: Oscar Niemeyer
This focal point of Brazil's new capital places the two national Congress chambers on a platform. Their opposing convex and concave circular forms with the dual administrative towers between them, result in the iconical silhouette of the city.

9

10

12

13

14

12-14 São Paulo, Memorial of the Latin American States, 1990
Architect: Oscar Niemeyer
The large urban site contains an assembly plaza with a symbolically bleeding open hand sculpture by Niemeyer. Crisp white freestanding buildings surround the space. Their long span concrete structures create an interactive sculptural totality.

594

15

16

15-18 Niteroi, Contemporary Art Museum, 1996
Architect: Oscar Niemeyer
Built on a peninsular reaching into Rio's harbour, the form and structure of this incredible building borders on the unbelievable. Prestressed radial interior ribs emanate from its central supporting hollow ring column. The upward sweep of the mushroom shaped glazed exterior wall runs parallel to the 'Sugarloaf' mountain in the distance.

19 São Paulo, Copan Building, 1951
Architect: Oscar Niemeyer
This co-operative apartment building takes on a wave-shaped plan form to fit onto the irregular inner city site. Two continuous horizontal louvres to each floor act as effective sun protection and afford privacy to the inhabitants.

17

18

Japan

The architecture of Japan was influenced historically by Chinese building practice, although many differences developed. Japan's humid and warm summer climate, as well as frequent earthquakes resulted in lightweight timber buildings raised off the ground that are resistant to earth tremors. The visual simplicity of important palace structures has had an influence on western architecture in the 20th Century. Elegant refinement and minimalist austere open interconnected spaces have influenced the modern architecture in much of the world, exemplified by the work of Mies Van der Rohe. Some of Frank Lloyd Wright's work has been influenced by Japan and conversely his multi-level entrance spaces in the Imperial Hotel in Tokyo has had an effect on modern Japanese architecture. Some parts of the lobby space has been reconstructed elsewhere in Japan after the Hotel's demolition in 1960.

After World War II great strides were made in modern Japanese architecture, not only in advanced technology, allowing earthquake resistant tall buildings, but expressing and infusing characteristics of traditional Japanese architecture in modern buildings.

The relationship between the restrained formal geometries of Japanese interiors is brought into a particular refined fusion with its landscape and garden architecture. A romantically peaceful serenity results.

1

1, 2 Kyoto, Katsura Palace, 1620-62
Architect: Kobori Enshu

4

5

3-5 Kyoto, Katsura Palace, 1663
Architect: Kobori Enshu
The masterpiece of serene simplicity is set in harmony with a picturesque landscape environment. The restrained minimalism of the timber building consists only of supporting columns and an open planned interior which can be subdivided, opened or closed to the outside with their sliding panels, to serve diverse uses.
The garden surroundings are contrived to idealise nature and brings water, stepping stones, paths and plants into a romantic scene of perfection.
The unornamented interiors are devoid of western furniture, with a bare geometric order created by the use of multiple tatami rice-straw floor mats.

6 Kyoto
Penelope, on our honeymoon, in December 1958, at a traditional inn. The floor is of equal size tatami mats and the thin sliding panels are of rice paper.

7

8

7, 8 Kyoto, Shishinden Imperial Palace, rebuilt 1855
The dominant concave roof covers a structure of equally spaced columns. Although the building is centuries old it is repaired and rebuilt periodically, seen in the façade of adjacent old and new timber columns.

9 Kyoto, The Golden Pavilion, 1397, rebuilt 1950's
The gilded shrine is built in a park surrounded by water. It exudes an atmosphere of untouchable perfection.

10

10 Kyoto, Heian Shrine, 1882
The large overhanging roof and widely
spaced columns mark the entrance to
a series of courtyards within.

**11, 13 Yokohama, Imperial Villa,
straddling a stream.**
The weathered timber old garden court
entrance gate.

12 Kyoto
A typical pagoda, a religious structure was
built following Chinese historic origins.

14 Nikko, Toshogu Shrine, 1636
A highly decorated building characteristic
of the "Baroque" period in Japanese
architecture.

12

13

15

16

17

15-17 Tokyo, The Imperial Hotel, 1916-1922 (demolished 1967)
Architect: Frank Lloyd Wright
Penelope and I stayed in the hotel just before its demolition. All interiors and furniture, designed by Wright, were still intact. The entrance hall was the most remarkable space in the huge complex. It had seven different levels, interacting spatially and all merging into the entrance foyer.
Built of brick and carved lava stone, the structure was supported on an ingenious system of driven piles, which saved the building in the disastrous 1923 earthquake.

18

18-20 Tokyo, Olympic Pool, 1964
Architect: Kenzo Tange
A unique structure of only two concrete
supports and a prestressed steel net
covering the concave roof.

19

22

23

21-22 Tokyo, Museum of Western Art, 1959

Architect: Le Corbusier

Suspended above an open ground floor, the plan of the museum is based on a "squared spiral". The focal area is a high top-lit space into which upper gallery floor balconies open, that in turn are lit through skylights above.

23 Tokyo, U.S. Embassy Apartments, 1951-52

Architects: Raymond & L. L. Rado

An early off-form concrete building with south facing continuous balconies to all living areas.

616

24

24, 25 Takamatsu, Kagawa Prefecture, 1955-58
Architect: Kenzo Tange
Solidly built of exposed textured concrete, the modern office building recalls traditional Japanese ponds with sculptural stone blocks.
The projecting concrete floor beams are reminiscent of early timber structures.

China

This ancient land enjoys a long history and great achievements with many architectural miracles such as "The Great Wall", built to protect the northern borders from predatory mountain people of the Steppes. The 6000 km long structure contains guard towers and Garrison towns. It is said to be the only man-made structure that is visible from the moon.

"The Forbidden City" contains the most impressive series of monumental structures interspersed with large courtyards connected by white marble stairs. The entry court is traversed by a wave shaped watercourse which generates a unique atmosphere in the vast open space.

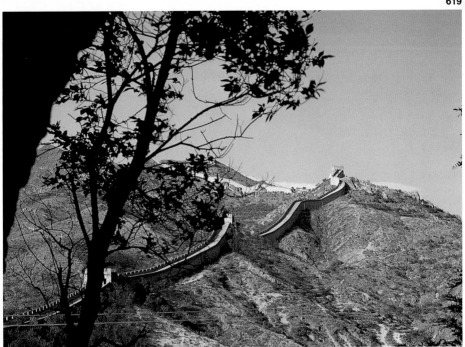

1

1, 2 Beijing, Great Wall of China.
Successive emperors ordered The Great
Wall of China to be constructed, protecting
the country from Northern Incursions. The
wall was started between the seventh to
the fifth centuries B.C. and was continuously strengthened over the ages to
become 7m high and wide, built on
an internal earth core, faced with brick
exteriors on a stone base. The huge wall,
some 6000 km long, winds up and down
across the mountainous landscape. Its
scale is unparalleled in the architecture of
fortifications.

3

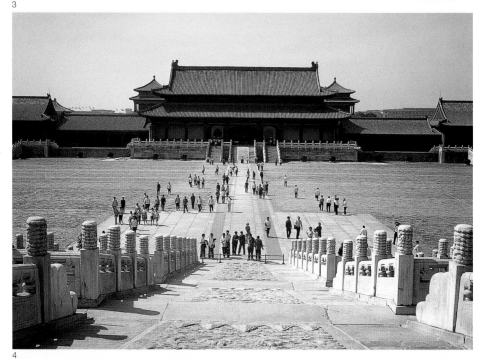

3-8 Beijing, The Forbidden City, 1403-20

This imperial palace housed the emperors from the fourteenth until the early twentieth centuries and consists of a virtual city with halls, pavilions and towers covering a walled compound of some 720,000 square metres, which takes more than half an hour to traverse. Buildings face a series of large courtyards interrupted by temple structures, residence halls and religious shrines. On my second visit, in 1977, new snow fell at night and offered a unique view of the first snow covered large court, the only space containing a curvilinear watercourse and stone foot bridges.

5

6

7

9

9 Hong Kong, Bank of China Tower, 1982-90

Architect: Ieoh Ming Pei

This landmark of the city has a triangulated exposed steel frame which expresses the three dimensional form of the structure.

10, 11 Beijing, Temple of Heaven

The colourful carved timber ceiling structure of the circular Temple of Heaven shrine.

Indonesia

Java, the central island of Indonesia, is the most architecturally fascinating and populous in the country of over 200 million people. It contains the finest remaining Hindu and Buddhist temple architecture of the seventh and tenth centuries.

Of the world's active volcanoes, 34% are in Indonesia. In the central area where once stood 240 temples most had collapsed. Reconstruction of them has been in progress since the 1930s.

1 Java, Parambanan

1

2-4 Java, Parambanan
The progress of restoring and rebuilding the temples in central Java is a slow task, that has lasted for decades and is still continuing. The blocks of dark volcanic stone have been collected and assembled with a number of temples completed. They are solid tall structures, only covered on the outside with decorative elaborate carvings and figures reusing the scattered stone blocks. Standing in the open landscape the visual impact of these monolithic tower structures is powerful.

3

4

5

6

5-8 Java, Borobudur

The most memorable of temples is the terraced solid stone square pyramid, with statues, relief carvings and "stupas" rising along continuously winding terraces and steep steps to the 34 metre high roof. The tallest inverted, 8 metre high stupa forms the top and is ringed with smaller perforated, inverted bell-like enclosures, each with a different gesture, sitting Buddha sculpture contained within.

7

8

India

The enduring achievements of Indian civilisation lie in its architecture. Built during the rule of various dominant cultures, Persian, Indian and Mughal styles merged in buildings of great refinements. These were often built centuries apart such as palaces, temples, forts, tombs, astrological observation structures and expansive town planning schemes. The most memorable of these were built during the powerful Mughal Empire in the 16th century, mainly located in northern India's Rajasthan, in Delhi and Agra.

The British influence in the 19th century produced grandiose government buildings. Mumbai (Bombay) remains today the preeminent Victorian gothic city in the world. New Delhi, was created as India's capital city by Lutyens in 1912, built in a hybrid of European and Indian architectural modes. In the early 1950's Le Corbusier was invited to undertake the planning and building of a huge new city, Chandigarh, in the Punjab, which had lost its capital, Lahore, during partition.

This immense undertaking can be compared to Brazil's capital Brasilia, both the successful totally planned new cities of the 20th century and both created by two of the era's greatest architects.

1 Agra Fort, Khass Mahal, 1565
This white marble pavilion housed the private apartments of the Emperor.

638

2

3

4

2 Agra, Taj Mahal
The detailed entry shows dark stone inlaid surfaces in the white marble exterior.

3, 4 Agra Fort
Carved marble surrounds the pool and scalloped arches support the pavilion.

5 Agra Fort
View from Agra Fort toward the Taj Mahal in the distance.

6 Agra, Taj Mahal, 1631-1657
Architect: Isa Khan
The mausoleum was constructed by Emperor Shah Jahan in memory of his deceased wife.
This world famous white marble iconic building has a graceful composition, arrangement of a central dome, towers and pointed arches, all raised on a podium and focused on an axial reflecting water-course.

7 Agra, Itimad Ud Daulah (The Small Taj), 1622-1628
This is the first white marble temple built with inlaid precious stones, foreshadowing the Taj Mahal, a building using beautiful geometric proportions and perforated stone grille exteriors.

5

8

9

10

11

8-10 New Delhi, Parliamentary Compound, 1912-30

Architects: Lutyens and Baker

A grand axial boulevard focuses on the domed Vice Regal Palace's formal gate, leading to the sumptuous multi-winged establishment.

Flanking both sides of the approach are government offices that have characteristic Indian Chattri pavilion projections with parasol shaped domed roofs.

The circular Parliament House, designed by Baker in 1930, is surrounded by a recessed colonnade above a solid stone base.

The atmosphere of this central government area is a grandiose imperial gesture, the final stage of the British Empire's rule in India.

11, 12 Jaipur, Hawa Mahal (Palace of the Winds), 1799

Architect: Maharaja Pratap Singh II

Jaipur's landmark is only a façade through which the city's main street can be over-looked with projecting honeycombed sandstone bays and half Chattri domed roofs.

13 Jaipur, Jantar Mantar (or Observatory), 1728

14-16 Jaipur, Jantar Mantar (or Observatory), 1728

Jantar Mantar was the Rajput Jai Singh's passion for astronomy. Covering a large open area are sculpture like structures from which positions of stars, altitudes and azimuths can be observed and eclipses calculated.

17, 18 Jaipur, City Palace, 18th Century

Located in the heart of the old city, a series of arched entries lead to courtyards, gardens and inner buildings, all with typical overhanging thin edged cornices and perforated stone screen façade infills.

15

16

17

18

19

20

19-21 Udaipur, Lake Palace, by Maharana Jagat Singh II, 1754

Located in the centre of Udaipur and built on an island in the lake, this formal royal palace must be the most romantic, superbly crafted and extravagant creation anywhere. Surrounded by stone arched pavilions facing the water, its central courtyards are filled with lotus ponds and swimming pools. The palace is now used as a luxury hotel.

22

22-30 Fatehpur Sikri, 1571-85
Capital of the Mughal Empire, Emperor Akbar.

This is among the finest cities built by edict of an Indian Emperor in the 16th century. The interlocking layout of various size open spaces, watercourses, ringed and punctuated by freestanding skilfully positioned structures, all provide constantly changing vistas as one strides through this amazing city. Built of durable red sandstone, some opposing white marble pavilions, perforated screens and fine workmanship, it is still something of a mystery why it was deserted so soon after its completion. The only explanation offered is the problem of water supply for its population. This cohesive complex creates a beautiful totality without equal.

25

26

27

28

29

30

31

33

31, 33 Amber Palace, 1592
Located high on a hillside overlooking a lake
below, this fortified compound was once
the ancient capital of Jaipur state.

32 Udaipur, City Palace, 1600-1725
The largest of Rajasthan's palace complexes
was built over long periods and yet retains
uniformity of design. Surmounted by terraces, balconies and towers, it offers fine
views over the lake.

34 Chandigarh, 1950-1985
Architect: Le Corbusier
The plan of the capital to the north of the
city shows the High Court, the Parliament
and the Secretariat with the open hand
sculpture and the Governor's palace to be
built later.
The housing districts for 150,000 people
was to be enlarged to 500,000 inhabitants.

35 Chandigarh
The Secretariat during construction, on
my first visit when I met Le Corbusier in
Chandigarh, in 1955. The towers attached
to the slab building contained access
ramps used for women labourers carrying
up buckets of concrete. The entire city was
built by hand.

36 Chandigarh
The Parliament building seen with the
foothills of the Himalayas in the distance.
The two chambers of government are in
the centre of the building, projecting far
above the roof and surrounded by circu-
lation space.
Offices are planned against the exterior
walls, covered with sun protection blades.

34

37

38

37-39 Chandigarh, The Parliament building

The dramatically upswept portico of the main entrance, with the Secretariat in the background, both reflect in the large water basins. The plan and cross section show the top lit continuously changing inner space around the chambers, which is the most beautiful of any of Le Corbusier's interiors.

40, 41, 43 The Secretariat building is 254 meters long and 42 meters high, with the ramped pedestrian access tower projecting from the façade. The continuous repetitive sun protected office galleries are interrupted by irregular height ministerial offices and formal meeting spaces, all of which, including the office's proportions, are based on Le Corbusier's modular system.

42, 44 The High Court building has an arched parasol-like roof structure which together with the brise-soliel along the ground floor courts protect the building from the heat. The open entrance portico leads between pylons toward winding ramps, that lead to upper floor offices. Great sculptured spaces result for the visitor.

41

42

43

44

45

47

48

45, 47 Ahmedabad, Shodhan House, 1951

Architect: Le Corbusier

Following the construction of Chandigarh, some industrialists in the city of Ahmedabad invited Le Corbusier to build houses and the headquarters of the Millowners organisation. The most dramatic of these is the Villa Shodhan, a 3 storey building of sculptural plasticity and penetrating spaces intertwining exteriors and interiors, with modular proportioned glass and solid infill walls.

46, 48 Ahmedabad, Sarabhai House, 1955

Architect: Le Corbusier

This ground level house is built of regular low concrete arches supported on regularly spaced beams on brick walls. The open interior in this tropical climate allows air currents across and longitudinally through the entire house. For the sons of the house a concrete slide allows their speedy descent into the swimming pool in the garden.

672

49

49, 50 Ahmedabad, Millowners' Association Building, 1954

Architect: Le Corbusier

Overlooking a river edge, the street approach leads over an inclined ramp into the open central space, to the offices and meeting halls. Both east and west facades are protected by brise-soleil from the strong sunlight. The form-boarded concrete gives a rugged texture to the entire structure.

51 Ahmedabad, Indian Institute of Management, 1963-74

Architect: Louis Kahn

This 65 acre campus accommodates all teaching areas, staff and student housing, in garden courts. The flat arched brick facades are tied with tensioned concrete lintels that give a distinctive form to the whole complex.

Thailand

Bangkok, the modern capital of Thailand, was founded in 1782 and consisted of encircling moats and walls which guarded the hinterland from the entrance of the main river.

King Rama V patronised European architecture and town planning which resulted in an amalgam of Victorian and Thai style structures.

The most remarkable assembly of such buildings are in the wall enclosed Grand Palace, used by the King for certain ceremonial occasions. Gold encrusted high pointed spire shrines, colourful sculptured figures and triple layered gabled religious pavilions create an astonishing group of buildings.

The tremendous reclining golden Buddha, 46 metres long and 15 metres high, is only one of 394 gilded Buddha images in temples and museums throughout Bangkok.

1-3 Bangkok, Grand Palace, 1782
The wall enclosed Grand Palace contains
Bangkok's glistening golden landmark; a
huge pointed spire shrine.

2

2 Angkor Wat
Entrance causeway with tower structures.

3, 4 Angkor Wat
Tower structure rising from courtyard and
ground plan showing central structures and
open courts.

3

1 Sydney, Hyde Park Barracks, 1817-19
Architect: Francis Greenway
A typical colonial brick building of fine
proportions following English Georgian
precedence.

**2 Sydney, Terrace House, mid 19th
Century**
Typical row house with shaded verandah
and English iron railings imported as ballast
on sailing ships.

3 Francis Greenway, 1777-1837

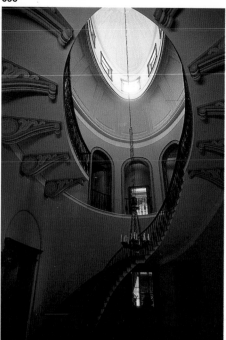

4

4 Sydney, Elizabeth Bay House, 1835
Architect: John Verge
Elegant house interior space reflecting
English Georgian taste.

5 Sydney, The Mint, 1814
Typical colonial era building with colonnaded verandahs.

6 Sydney, Terrace Houses, late 19th Century
Typical stepping up continuous terrace
row houses representative of hilly inner
districts of the city. Brick cross walls
support timber floors and slate roofs. The
narrow allotments have private enclosed
rear gardens.

7 Sydney, Opera House, 1957-73
Architect: Jørn Utzon
Selected at an international architectural
competition, this unique precast concrete
ribbed structure is covered with glazed
white tiles. After structural completion
a dispute with the newly elected state
government client, the architect was
dimissed in 1966, never to return. The
building was completed by others and
resulted in disappointing interiors. The
exterior Opera House design is considered
the very icon of Australia.

5

6

Biography

Harry Seidler, considered one of Australia's foremost architects was born in 1923 in Vienna Austria. Following the anschluss occupation in 1938 he fled to England where, after the outbreak of war in 1940, he was interned as an enemy alien. During his internment he was transported to Quebec Canada, and almost two years later he was released to study architecture at the University of Manitoba.

In 1945-6 he attended the Master's class at Harvard University as a student of Walter Gropius. He later studied design under Josef Albers at Black Mountain College. He worked with Marcel Breuer in New York (1946-48) and with Oscar Niemeyer in Brazil on his way to Australia in 1948.

He went to Australia to build a house for his parents; the 'Rose Seidler House' in Sydney 1950, which is now a house museum owned and operated by the Historic Houses Trust of NSW.

During over fifty years of practice he has built a great variety of work from houses to sky-scrapers, both in Australian cities and inter-nationally. His work has been widely pub-lished and he has won many awards inclu-ding the RIBA Gold Medal in 1996. He has taught and lectured extensively. His most recent works include a housing community beside the Danube in Vienna.

During his many travels to his various inter-national projects, Seidler developed a love of photography to document what he con-sidered to be the peak achievements of architecture throughout the ages.

This is the first book of his photography. Seidler's work is not illustrated in this book. For a pictorial record see www.seidler.net.au